THE RISE AND FALL OF ECONOMIC JUSTICE

The Rise and Fall of Economic Justice and Other Papers

C. B. MACPHERSON

Oxford New York
OXFORD UNIVERSITY PRESS
1985

Oxford University Press, Walton Street, Oxford OX2 6DP

London New York Toronto
Delhi Bombay Calcutta Madras Karachi
Kuala Lumpur Singapore Hong Kong Tokyo
Nairobi Dar es Salaam Cape Town
Melbourne Auckland
and associated companies in
Beirut Berlin Ibadan Mexico City Nicosia

Oxford is a trade mark of Oxford University Press

British Library Cataloguing in Publication Data
Macpherson, C. B.
The rise and fall of economic justice and
other papers.
1. Democracy
I. Title
321.8   JC423
ISBN 0-19-215360-9

Library of Congress Cataloging in Publication Data
Macpherson, C. B. (Crawford Brough), 1911-
The rise and fall of economic justice, and other papers.
Contents: The rise and fall of economic justice—Problems of human rights
in the late twentieth century—The prospects of economic and
industrial democracy—[etc.]
1. Distributive justice—Addresses, essays, lectures.
2. Civil rights—Addresses, essays, lectures. 3. Industrial
management—Employee participation—Addresses, essays, lectures.
4. Property—Addresses, essays, lectures. 5. Liberalism—Addresses,
essays, lectures. 6. Economics—Political aspects—
Addresses, essays, lectures. I. Title.
HB523.M35 1985   323.4'6   84-27170
ISBN 0-19-215360-9

Set by DMB (Typesetting)
Printed in Great Britain by
St Edmundsbury Press, Bury St Edmunds, Suffolk

PREFACE

This volume presents four new papers and eight papers previously published. Although the papers range widely in subject matter, the critic who remarked that I never write about anything except possessive individualism will here find no need to retract. All the papers are concerned in one way or another with state, class, and property—the essential constitutents of the theory of possessive individualism. All but the last three papers are comparative and historical: each of the last three deals with only one theory, or one school of theory, but even they have comparative and historical dimensions.

CONTENTS

ACKNOWLEDGEMENTS

My thanks are due to the editors and publishers of the following journals and books in which the papers listed were first published: *European Journal of Sociology* (for Chapter 5, 1977); *Dissent* (for Chapter 6, 1977); Wilfrid Laurier University Press, Waterloo, Canada (for Chapter 7) in *Theories of Property: Aristotle to the Present*, edited by Anthony Parel and Thomas Flanagan, 1979); *Economic and Industrial Democracy* (for Chapter 8, 1980); *Journal of the History of Ideas* (for Chapter 9, 1978); Cambridge University Press (for Chapter 10, in *After Marx*, edited by Terence Ball and James Farr, 1984); *Philosophical Forum* (for Chapter 11, 1983); *Political Studies* (for Chapter 12, 1977).

CHAPTER 1

The Rise and Fall of Economic Justice

This chapter is an enquiry into the probable future of the concept of economic justice. Any such enquiry must be speculative, but the speculation will not be wholly random if it is grounded in history: more precisely, grounded in some analysis of the relation, down to the present, between the changing fortunes of the concept and changes in prevailing economic and social relations. I shall show that the concept arose rather late in the history of human society, that it fell virtually to extinction a few centuries ago, and that it has revived somewhat in our century.

As we trace that rise and fall and revival, some correlations between them and certain clearly discernible changes in the society and the economy will appear. And there will be reason to think that those relations are not merely empirical correlations, but also causal relations: it will appear that social and economic changes sometimes compelled, and sometimes were compelled by, a change in the status of the concept. It may even appear that there is a dialectical relation between them: at least, there is some reason to think that the social forces which produced the present revival of the concept were a necessary outcome of the economic changes which produced the previous fall of the concept. However that may be, a look at the history of the concept should help us with our main question: whether or not the presently revived concept is likely to have a long life. I shall suggest, not.

I shall begin by arguing:

(a) that the idea of economic justice arose only when market-determined systems of production and distribution encroached on politically determined ones, which is to say, long after the emergence of private property, class division, and the state;

(b) that it arose then as a defensive action against the encroachment of the market on traditional political society;

(c) that when, in the seventeenth and eighteenth centuries, the market triumphed in our Western societies, the very idea of economic justice was consigned to oblivion by the mainstream political thinkers as being incompatible with market determination of values and entitlements, and from then till the mid-nineteenth century survived only in a handful of radical thinkers and working-class movements; and

(d) that intermittent attempts of liberal thinkers from the mid-nineteenth century to the present to revive the concept of economic justice have been unable to establish a theoretical foothold for it because they have still relied on the allocative market whose supremacy the concept was designed to prevent.

I shall then notice that, in spite of this, the concept is widely used in the political *practice* of the Western liberal democracies in the twentieth century, and shall enquire what forces brought about that practical revival, and whether they are likely to sustain it.

1. Definition

Let me begin by offering a provisional definition of the concept of economic justice, sufficient to distinguish it from justice in general and to set out its bare essentials. Something like that seems necessary, for one cannot simply point to the most evident examples of the concept, which are classical and medieval, and say: look at Aristotle and Aquinas if you want to know what the concept is. That would still leave the question, what is to count as a concept of economic justice at any later time? We need to know this if we are to look at its prospects in our own time.

One obvious requirement of a concept of economic justice is that it be about *economic* relations, that is, relations into which people enter, in any society, in their capacities as producers or owners or exchangers of valuable goods or services. And if economic justice is to be treated as a distinct branch of justice, economic relations must be seen as having become something distinct from social and political relations in general, that is, as something no longer automatically given by, or engulfed in, a prevailing social or political order.

A second requirement, no less evident I think, is that a concept of economic justice always asserts a claim to regulate economic relations in the light of some ethical principle. Economic justice, like justice in general, is nothing if not a value-laden concept.

Provisionally then, I define the concept of economic justice by two stipulations: (1) it treats economic relations as having become distinct from social relations in general, and now requiring principles more specific than those of justice in general; and (2) it seeks to impose on economic relations some ethical principle deduced from natural law (or divine law) or from a supposed social nature of man. Notice that I do not say from *any* supposed nature of man but only from a supposed *social* nature of man. For a theory which, like Hobbes's or the social Darwinists', starts from a postulate of an essentially unsocial nature of man, is left without any ethical principle that could override the economic behaviour logically required of unsocial man, i.e. pure individual maximizing behaviour, either in the market or by open force.

It may be objected that my second stipulation is too narrow. Why, it may be asked, should we rule out (as that stipulation does) Hobbes's concept of justice in economic relations as simply the keeping of contracts 'in buying, and selling; hiring and letting to hire; lending, and borrowing; exchanging, bartering, and other acts of contract'?[1] I defend my stipulation, with its exclusion of such a concept from the category of economic justice, on the ground that such a concept puts economic relations out of the control of any purposeful human agency, and removes them from any possibility of being judged by any ethical criterion.

2. The Late Arrival of Economic Justice

The earliest societies about which there is documentary evidence (to say nothing of still earlier societies, of which we have only debatable anthropological speculation) show no signs of having had a concept of economic justice. The Mosaic Law (*c*.15th cent. BC), was formulated for a pastoral and simple agricultural society where there was already private property in land and its produce, and in houses, flocks, cattle, draft animals, and bond-servants, and some use of gold and silver as money. The Mosaic Law prohibited theft, covetousness, and false weights and measures; prescribed fair treatment of hired servants, and protection for escaped bond servants; and regulated debts and usury; but in all this there was nothing that we should recognize as a concept of economic justice. The high civilizations of the Middle Eastern empires and kingdoms in the third and second millennia BC, which were based on settled agriculture and which sustained extensive commerce and a substantial merchant class, had more elaborate legal codes, such as the Code of Hammurabi (Babylon, *c*.1750 BC) with its detailed laws concerning contracts of sale, lease, mortgage, etc., but also lacked any recognizable notion of economic justice. Any contracts were just, if freely entered into.

---

[1] *Leviathan*, Ch. 15 (p. 208 in the Penguin edition, ed. C. B. Macpherson).

In both cases the reason is evident. What we now call economic relations, and think of as something separate from all the other relations that make up a society, were not then seen as separate. Who should get what of the material means of life, and who should contribute what labour to their production, were both determined by one's place in the tribal or imperial society. One's place in the productive process was simply given by one's place in the society. The relations of production were the political relations of the society. Both were given by the level of felt wants and the level of techniques available to meet them. No one separated out the productive (and exchange) arrangements from the social and political arrangements. The relations of production and exchange were encompassed in the overriding social and political relations.

Thus we cannot, on the record, locate the emergence of a distinct idea of economic justice as far back in time as the appearance of private property and slavery or the appearance, in addition to that, of extensive commerce, markets, money, and a merchant class. The early markets, extensive as they were, were subsidiary to the main sinews of the society and state. And what is more important, they were controlled by the state, for the purposes and designs of the state: they were thus sufficiently governed by custom or by legal codes imposed by the authority of a mouthpiece of the gods or God (as in the Hebrew scriptures) or by a god-king (as in the Middle Eastern empires and kingdoms). The markets did not determine prices: trade was carried on at prices or equivalencies fixed by the state.

The turning-point is not the emergence of markets and merchants, much less of private property and slavery. It is the achievement by merchants and markets of a relative autonomy or independence from the state. Only then did upholders of the values of customary societies have to begin to fight back against the inroads of money and markets on an older way of life. Only when those inroads could be seen to be dissolving the old ways was it necessary to mount an ideological defensive action. And the only way to mount it was to look at the new economic order as something threatening to, and hence separate from, the traditional order sanctified by tribal or community custom or imperial customary law. To do this required, for the first time in history, a concept of *economic* justice distinct from the general notion of justice.

The turning-point did not come for many centuries. When the Bronze Age gave way to the Iron Age (from about 1200 BC) a way was opened for a significant change in the relations of production and exchange. As knowledge of iron-smelting spread, there was a much enlarged class of

craftsmen making everyday tools for the primary producers, a consequent growth of production of these commodities for the market
rather than the household or the village community or the palace,
leading to the replacement of the village commune by aggregations of
independent commodity producers for an impersonal market, and of
course, to the growth of money transactions, which now began to
permeate local, as they had previously permeated long-distance, trade.

But the pace of change in those centuries was slower than we are used
to, and the rise and fall of empires alternating with simpler societies
leaves us no straight line of evolution. However, the change to an increasingly impersonal market economy was bound to have a dissolvent effect
on either an imperial or a simpler society.

The first record we have of such an invasion of an old order by mercantile markets is in classical Greece, at the period when, with merchants'
wealth increasing, the poorer primary producers were impoverished
and sold up, the merchant class sought to take control of the state from
the old ruling class, and a menaced or impoverished peasantry became
a threat to any social order. This is the classic *stasis* or endemic civil war
of which we read in Plato and Aristotle. It appeared first in the sixth
century BC, where Solon's reforms were designed, but failed, to remedy
it. This is still far from what we know as *capitalist* relations of production: money capital had not yet seized on the whole productive process
by turning the primary producer's labour, as well as their produce, into
a market commodity. But the accumulative monetary market system
had gone far enough by Solon's time to demand counteraction. And the
rot had set in far enough that the counteraction had to be ideological as
well as political. It called for a concept of economic justice, comprising
principles both of fair exchange of commodities and of fair distribution
of the society's whole product.

The concept of economic justice gets its first clear presentation in the
fourth century BC, by Aristotle. In the time scale of human societies, the
fourth century BC is distinctly at the modern end. But it was only then
that the idea of economic justice as a problem requiring separate attention arose. The more ancient civilizations, in which the market had not
been, or even threatened to be, an autonomous organizing mechanism
of production and exchange, had not needed any such concept. There is
no record of any speculation, in the Bronze Age empires and kingdoms,
of any such notions of economic justice.

Aristotle was the first to make the distinction between, on the one
hand the household or simple market economy in which production and

exchange were for use, and on the other hand a more advanced market economy in which exchange was initiated by the merchant using his money capital to buy in order to sell at a profit and thus to increase his wealth, a system in which 'money is the starting-point and the goal of exchange.' He saw that his own society had moved well along the road from the simple to the advanced market economy. And he made a strong ethical case that the latter was destructive of the good life. He called it unnatural, on three grounds: it makes acquisition the goal instead of merely a means of the good life; the accumulation process is without limit whereas the good life requires only limited material wealth; and it is a means by which some men gain at the expense of others, which is unjust.

There are also in Aristotle's doctrine the beginnings of the two branches of the concept of economic justice that were more jully developed in medieval Europe, i.e. commutative and distributive justice. Commutative justice—justice in acts of exchange—requires that they be at a 'just price'. This was not too clearly defined, but seems to have been that which is not disruptive of traditional standards which hold society together. The just price is that which yields to the producer of each commodity a return proportionate to the status customarily enjoyed by a person of his occupation or skill. The ratios, that is to say the prices, were to be socially determined, not left to the determination of the market. The concern was with how much produce, i.e. how much of the material means of life, each exchanger got in return for his produce or labour.

Distributive justice—justice in the distribution of society's whole product among the citizens, required at least that every household should have the moderate income needed for the good life, the amount that enabled each to combine temperance with liberality. Distributive, like commutative, justice was concerned with the outcome of the new relations of *exchange* brought by the rise of merchant capital: the relations of *production*, whether by slave labour or by free peasants and craftsmen, were taken as given. Aristotle's concern with the accumulation of *wealth* by the merchants, was because it altered the relations of exchange and hence the distribution of *income*: it imperilled the livelihood, the material means of consumption, of the free citizens.

In all this, Aristotle can be seen to be applying, to a fairly advanced market society, moral standards drawn from an earlier traditional society. He failed to persuade the rulers or the citizens to turn away from the accumulative market, but no clearer case for their doing so could have been made. He was quite right in seeing that the root of the difficulties of the Greek city-states was that the market had got free from customary social bonds, and it was a reasonable inference that the best chance of holding off a market takeover, i.e. a takeover by a commercial class and a commercial morality, and holding onto traditional society, was to create and press an idea of specifically economic justice. To the extent that the growth of market behaviour had separated the economy from the society it was necessary to set up a separate concept of justice in the economy.

When Aristotle's writings were rediscovered in Western Europe in the twelfth century AD, the then established European feudal society was already under the same sort, though not yet the same degree, of pressure from market encroachments as his society had been in his time. So it is not surprising that the outstanding theorist of the thirteenth century—St. Thomas Aquinas—devoted explicit attention to problems of economic justice and produced a quite similar doctrine. Commutative justice required that things exchanged should be of equal value, otherwise one party to the exchange was cheated. The just price was that which gave each producer a return for his labour appropriate to his rank and skill. On the justice of merchants' gain from selling at a higher price than buying, Aquinas was seemingly more lenient than Aristotle. Trade for gain was allowed as just if the gain did not exceed a suitable return for the merchant's labour, the risks he took, and the costs of transportation. But it is significant that the ground on which this was allowed was that such trade might be beneficial to the household and to the community. The justice of trading for gain depended on the gain being moderate by customary standards and on the trade being potentially beneficial to the household or the community.

The medieval limitations on trade (which included a prohibition of usury and of monopolistic market-rigging) were not, as later theorists took them to be, perverse limitations on some innate propensity of the individual to 'truck, barter, and exchange one thing for another' as Adam Smith put it. They were, rather, outcomes of the value systems of societies not yet transformed by the market, societies in which the organization of production and exchange was subjected to social goals. They were defence mechanisms against a complete market take-over. A distinction was made between two kinds of exchange activities, and of the gains arising from them. Gains made by moving commodities from less-wanted to more-wanted areas were ethically unexceptionable: they took advantage merely of geographical terms of trade, and were beneficial to both parties, Gains made by taking advantage of a superior bargaining position, as in usury and monopolistic price fixing, were proscribed: they took advantage of differential power, and were at the expense of the weaker party. These principles of economic justice, with all the power of the Church behind them, had some success, until the end of the Middle Ages, in preventing the market escaping the bonds of traditional social order. But in the end they proved powerless.

3. The Decline and Fall of Economic Justice

As the feudal order succumbed to the mercantile state in country after country in Europe from the fifteenth and sixteenth centuries on, the medieval doctrine of economic justice also succumbed. That was only to be expected. But the striking thing is that the medieval doctrine was not replaced by any new theory of economic justice. Universal ethical standards sank under national interest standards. Ethical debate sank in the seventeenth century into mercantilist controversies, in which it was taken for granted both that the national interest should be the goal and hence the criterion of the good, and that the nation's economic life should be directed by the state rather than being left entirely to the free play of entrepreneurs in the market.

This may sound like a reversion to the idea that the economy should be subordinate to the maintenance of the traditional fabric of society, now as represented by the national state. But there was a very great difference. It was not the traditional fabric, but the new fabric of a mercantile society, that the state was to promote. Now the national interest was assumed to be the accumulation and exertion of private and corporate capitals. It was market motivations that were relied on to build the strength of the nation. The debate was now mainly whether state policy should be directed towards the accumulation of gold and silver or towards other means of stimulating capital accumulation and a more advanced level of economic activity. It no longer mattered whether the great gain brought, for instance, to England by the operations of chartered overseas trading bodies was the result of their taking advantage merely of geographical differences in the values ascribed to different commodities in the East and West (which would have been justified by the medieval doctrine), or to their exerting superior power to impose terms of trade favourable to themselves (which would not have been justified by the older principle). Considerations of economic justice did not enter into the policy question.

The death of the concept of economic justice may be said to have been proclaimed by Thomas Hobbes in 1651. Although he was no friend of the rising mercantile order, he saw that it had come to stay. Accordingly, he dismissed the claims of both commutative and distributive justice as irrelevant.

Commutative justice required that exchanges be of things of equal value. But as Hobbes saw it, 'the value of all things contracted for, is measured by the Appetite of the Contractors: and therefore the just value, is that which they be contented to give.'[2] All market exchanges are therefore, by definition, exchanges of equal values, that is, values deemed equal by the exchangers.

Distributive justice required that a society's produce should be distributed in proportion to men's merits. But in a full-market society there is no measure of a man's merit other than what the market will award him: as Hobbes put it, 'the Value or Worth of a man, is as of all other things, his Price; that is to say, so much as would be given for the use of his Power . . .'[3] So any actual distribution is by definition a distribution in proportion to men's merits, and hence just; it cannot be judged by any non-market standard.

Hobbes set the tone of all subsequent liberal theories. Locke, agreeing with Hobbes in this as in so much else, was quite clear in his own mind that the market price was the just price, and he went into still more detail in asserting that any particular parcel of commodities could justly be sold by the same merchant at different prices in different markets at the same time.[4]

Economic justice disappeared as a category of political and economic theory. It is not difficult to see why this happened then. For only then in the most advanced countries had the market changed, and was seen to have changed, qualitatively: human energies and skills—men's ability to work productively—became normally marketable and marketed. From then on, an increasing part of the whole working population sold their labour power rather than their products. Labour itself, as Hobbes saw, had become a commodity, the price of which was determined by the impersonal market.[5] The sway of the market was thus potentially complete: the relative autonomy of the market from society and traditional socially imposed norms was assured.

[2] *Leviathan*, Ch. 15, p. 208.
[3] *Leviathan*, Ch. 10, p. 151.
[4] John Locke: MS note 'Venditio' (1695), reproduced in full in John Dunn, 'Justice and Locke's Political Theory', *Political Studies*, Feb. 1968, pp. 84-7.
[5] *Leviathan*, Ch. 24, p. 295.

There were some rearguard actions by custodians of traditional social values. In England, Tudor and Stuart governments tried to limit the market takeover by limitations on land enclosures, by regulation of wages and labour contracts, and by provisions to protect the work force from the worst effects of market fluctuations. Provisions of the latter sort continued into the nineteenth century, until swept away by the Poor Law Reform of 1834. But in the mainstream of both political theory and political economy, from the seventeenth century on, there was no more concern with economic justice.

Some radical theorists in the early nineteenth century, notably the so-called Ricardian socialists (Hodgskin, Thompson, Bray) writing in the 1820s and 1830s, did argue in terms of economic justice, tracing distributive injustice to commutative injustice.[6] And by 1875 the German social democrats, in their Gotha Programme, put their case mainly in terms of distributive justice. But the most radical theorist of the century, Marx, held that all of that theory was fundamentally misguided precisely beause it looked only at *distributive* relations, or the sphere of circulation or exchange, and not at the relations of *production*. His sharpest complaint about the 'vulgar socialists' was their concentration on the distribution of income ('the means of consumption') instead of the way the consumable income was produced under capitalism. Demands for 'equitable distribution' of the whole social product were empty: 'Does not the bourgeoisie consider that the present distribution is equitable? And is it not in fact the only "equitable" distribution on the basis of the present method of production?' Again: 'Vulgar Socialism (and with it a section of the Democrats) has taken over from bourgeois economics the method of treating and considering distribution as independent of the methods of production and thereby representing Socialism as turning principally on distribution.[7] This, for Marx, was a dangerous mistake: the drive should not be for a just distribution of income but for new relations of production, since they determined both the distribution of income and the possibility of a transformation of the human condition.

The socialist movement, Marx held, should certainly seek to increase the workers' share at the expense of the capitalists, but it should not delude itself by talk about equitable distribution. To make distributive

[6] See below, p. 13; cf. Cheney C. Ryan, 'Socialist Justice and the Right to the Labor Product', *Political Theory VIII.* 4 (1980).

[7] Karl Marx, *Critique of the Gotha Programme* (1875) (New York, International Publishers, 1933), pp. 26, 32-3.

justice the centrepiece of the socialists' demands (as the Lasalleans, in their Gotha Programme, were doing) was to play into the hands of the capitalists, who could reasonably (on Marx's own analysis) claim that there was nothing unjust or inequitable in the capitalists' taking the surplus value that accrued to them from their buying labour power at its market value and benefitting from that purchase.[8]

That Marx thought it necessary to downgrade distributive justice[9] does however show that at least the moderate German social-democratic movement by 1875 was putting its case in terms of economic justice. And as we shall notice, social-democratic and labour parties, and the labour movement generally in the West, have pressed their claims largely in those terms since then. The revival of economic justice, though not at a very profound theoretical level, came first from working-class practice.

Liberal mainstream theory—both political economy and political theory—has remained largely impervious to a concept of economic justice from the eighteenth century to the present. The classical political economists of the eighteenth and nineteenth centuries were indeed interested in analysing what determined the distribution of the annual produce of a nation as between landowners, capitalist entrepreneurs, and workers, but since they believed that what the freely competitive market did, or could do, was all for the best, they did not discuss the distribution in terms of justice. Later in the nineteenth century, as political economy turned into modern economics, it abandoned even an interest in the market determination of class distribution.

It is true that in liberal-democratic political theory, distributive justice has shown signs of revival intermittently since the mid-nineteeth century, but for reasons we shall see, it has never taken root. John Stuart Mill was shocked by the injustice of the distribution of wealth in his society, but since he attributed that distribution, not to the operation of the capitalist market, but to extraneous institutions, and since he still relied on competitive markets and a virtually unlimited property right,

[8] For an elaborate discussion of Marx's position on economic justice, see the controversy between Allen Wood and Z. I. Husami, in *Philosophy and Public Affairs*, I. 3 (Spring 1972), VIII. 1 (1978), and VIII. 3 (1979).

[9] G. A. Cohen ('Freedom, Justice and Capitalism', *New Left Review* 126 (Mar-Apr 1981), 13, n.7) has pointed out that Marx was here objecting only to the social democrats' failure to see that the distribution of income (the means of consumption) was an automatic result of the distribution of capital and land (the material means of production), and has concluded that Marx cannot be said to have been hostile to the whole idea of justice in distribution. True enough, but it is still fair to say that Marx downgraded the concept of distributive justice, for that concept has been, ever since Aristotle, mainly confined to the distribution of the means of consumption.

he could not establish a new foothold for a concept of distributive justice which would counteract the market distribution. In any case, distributive justice was never as important for Mill as were individual liberty and the improvement of mankind. Liberal theorists in the idealist tradition, such as T. H. Green, also made little of economic justice. What shocked Green was not so much the distributive injustice of late-nineteenth-century capitalism as its debasing of the human essence by preventing so many from coming within reach of the 'moral vocation' of man; and Green, like Mill, could see no alternative to the market.

Later liberal theorists have generally let the idea of economic justice go by default, since they also have relied on the market, though calling for some state action to offset its worst allocative effects. The most acclaimed theory of justice in our own time, that of John Rawls, is devoted to working out a general principle of distribution which will justify the class difference in life prospects which any market society (indeed, he argues, any society) is bound to produce. His is certainly a general theory of distributive justice. But it is scarcely recognizable as a theory of *economic* justice. For it starts from the claims of dissociated individuals, not of individuals as members of society, and assumes market-maximizing behaviour as their innate or essential attribute, whereas the hallmark of the concept of economic justice has been its assumption that social norms and ethical values should prevail over, or not be eroded by, impersonal market values.

It might be argued that Rawls's theory does meet the criteria for a theory of economic justice, since it does propose to subject distributive arrangements to an ethical principle. But I do not think such an argument can be sustained. For Rawls sets a severe limit to the amount of redistribution of income allowed by his ethical principle, and the limit is dictated by the market economy.

His ethical distributive principle does not permit an increase of welfare-state redistribution to a point at which 'greater taxes interfere so much with economic efficiency that the prospects of the least advantaged in the present generation are no longer improved but begin to decline.[10] The test of economic efficiency is to be applied explicitly in 'the competitive economy',[11] and it logically must be a completely market-dominated one in which the negative response of entrepreneurs to increases in taxation reduces the productivity of the whole economy. It is the classical model of the competitive capitalist market economy, in

10 John Rawls, *A Theory of Justice*, (Harvard University Press, 1971), p. 286.
11 *Ibid.*, p. 284.

which impersonal market forces determine investment and productivity. Thus Rawls's ethical distributive principle does not prevail over, but is overridden by, the capitalist market relations of production. And indeed this is the only position consistent with his fundamental Hobbesian assumption of unsocial maximizing individuals as the irreducible units of modern society.

We may conclude that the distributive component of the concept of economic justice has not been effectively revived in liberal, or accepted in Marxian, political theory.

The notion of commutative justice made even less of a comeback. It remained of no interest to the liberal theorists. Something like it did reappear, early in the nineteenth century in the writings of the Ricardian socialists, who held that it was through *exchanges* of unequal values that the working class was exploited. Their measure of equal value was equal labour input. They thought in terms of homogeneous labour, not the ranked labour of the medieval doctrine: they appealed not to a traditional heirarchical social order, but to a vision of a classless society. Not surprisingly, this made no impression on mainstream liberal political theory. Marx too rejected it, for much the same reason as he rejected the distributive justice concept of the Gotha Programme: both concepts focused on the sphere of circulation rather than on the fundamental relations of production. So commutative justice also got no foothold in nineteenth-century theory.

Thus the whole concept of economic justice seemed, by the nineteenth century, to have been knocked out of the running, or at least permanently crippled. The reason is plain: in the measure that the capitalist market economy triumphed, it rendered the old notions of distributive and commutative justice helpless and useless: they could no longer be used to fight the market takeover.

The reason for their failure may be put in another way. I said earlier that a concept of economic justice distinct from justice in general required that economic relations be seen as having become distinct from (that is, not engulfed in) social and political relations in general. That was a requirement for the historical *emergence* of the concept. We may now add that that is only a special case. The logical requirement for the *existence* of the concept is not only that the economic relations not be engulfed in the social and political relations, but also that the former must not engulf the latter. But that is just what they did in the seventeenth and eighteen centuries. The relations of the market superseded all other relations. Critics on the left and on the right lamented, in the nineteenth century, that the cash nexus had replaced all traditional social relations, and the received wisdom was that status had given way to contract. Economic relations became again indistinguishable from social and political relations, but now because they had swallowed them up. Not only did economic justice disappear: justice in general was reduced to, where it was not displaced by, market calculation of maximum utility, or the keeping of contracts. As long as the capitalist market economy was generally accepted as on balance beneficial, there was scarcely any use for a concept of justice at all, and little thought was given to it in mainstream theory.

4. The Revival of Economic Justice

It will now not be difficult to see how and why there has been in our century a revival of the concept of economic justice. The revival matches a decline of confidence in the beneficence, and indeed in the possibility, of a freely competitive capitalist market economy. The decline of confidence has been more evident among uninstructed voters than among political and economic theorists. Accordingly, the revival of the concept has been in the political practice, rather than in the political theory, of the liberal democracies. But theory may catch up, so we should notice and try to explain the change in practice.

There is no doubt that the concepts of distributive and commutative justice have reappeared in the political practice of the liberal democracies in the twentieth century. Distributive justice, which we saw used by social-democratic parties from the late nineteenth century on, became still more widely used in the twentieth century. All political parties took to putting their case in terms of distributive justice. Government policies were defended, and attacked, on that ground. Elections were mainly fought on it, at least until very recently, although now the main issue is more often economic recovery or avoidance of economic disaster: the implications of that shift we shall notice shortly. The idea of commutative justice, or something like it, has also reappeared in such things as consumer protection legislation and the judicial doctrine of 'unconscionable' contracts.

If we are to consider the probable duration of these revivals we must look more closely at the forces which led to them. Three twentieth-century changes in Western society, each of them produced by the logic of capitalism, may be identified as the main forces.

Most obvious is the growth of trade unions, and labour and social-democratic parties, to the strength which brought the welfare-state measures typical of every advanced capitalist democracy. Since those measures were and are demanded in the name of economic justice, their arrival put economic justice on the agenda of all political parties.

A second change in the nature of the capitalist economy in the twentieth century was the decline of market competition in face of concentrations of capital which, in more and more sectors of the economy, let a few very large corporations dominate the market. When corporate capitals become so large that they can control markets instead of being controlled by them, it can no longer be said that the market automatically treats buyers and sellers equally, or that every exchange is by definition a just exchange. Thus, with the twentieth-century decline of competition, the market could no longer claim exemption from non-market ethical standards: the way was opened for some revival of commutative justice.

A third change, less obvious but no less important, is that the market is no longer expected, and no longer allowed, to do the whole job of allocation of rewards. The market no longer does the whole job of distribution of the total annual product between all those who may be said to have contributed to its production. In every advanced capitalist country, the state now intervenes in many ways in that allocation: the state prevents or distorts the allocation which the market would have made. The present allocation is indeed still done largely *through* markets, but it is not done *by* markets: the part that is done through markets is done by state and corporate power blocs operating in markets, not by autonomous markets.

The state has been compelled to intervene, partly by pressure from organized labour, partly by pressure from various sections of organized capital, and partly by the need to save the system from itself. These pressures continue. They indicate that the market by itself is widely regarded by the most advanced sections of capital, as well as by organized labour (and farmers), as incompetent to look after a fair allocation of rewards. So in this respect also, the market can no longer claim exemption from non-market ethical standards. Moreover, the state, which now shares the allocative function, must, in so far as it is a democratic state, claim that its economic policies are based on the public interest; and the most convenient, because most familiar, principle for the state to invoke is economic justice.

If these are the reasons why wide use is now being made of the notion of economic justice, how durable is that use likely to be? What are the long-term prospects of the concept? We may look in turn at distributive and commutative justice.

5. The Probable Future of Economic Justice

(i) *Distributive justice*

Given a continuing enlargement of the state's allocative and regulatory functions, and a continuing increase in the strength of the monopolistic or oligopolistic corporate sector, both of which tendencies may reasonably be presumed, what can we expect?

One possibility is such an alliance between corporate capital and the regulatory state as would negate social-democratic pressures by effectively destroying the democratic process. Such a corporatist or plebiscitarian state would neither have to accede to demands for distributive justice nor need to defend itself in those terms. It would appeal instead to other values—efficiency and stability. It would, indeed it already does, hold itself out as the only mechanism capable of saving the country from economic collapse—from massive unemployment and runaway inflation, which together are more to be feared than a little economic injustice. When calamity threatens, the distribution of misery becomes unimportant. The claims of distributive justice would be buried. That this is no fanciful possibility is suggested by the electoral success which right-wing parties have had in recent times in putting economic efficiency and stability ahead of distributive questions.

A second possibility, at the other extreme, is that the contest between democratic pressures and vested interests might go the other way. If democracy is not put down, democratic forces might take control of the capitalist state and transcend or transform our present managed capitalism. It is not impossible that such forces should be generated, both within sections of the working class who become convinced of the incompetence of managed capitalism and become resentful of their role as mere counters manipulated by impalpable power centres, and within a middle class increasingly aware of the deteriorating quality of life under late capitalism.

Supposing such a transformed society to have been brought into existence, would the concept of distributive justice have a continued lease of life? Not for long, I think. For such a transformed society is unlikely to be achieved by pressures which rely, as trade unions and social-democratic parties traditionally have done, mainly on making their case on grounds of distributive justice. By the time such a transformed society was reached, the main concern of the movements which had brought it into being, and which presumably would give it its direction, would no longer be distributive justice. Priority would have been given to other values, which may be summed up as quality of life: not merely the quality of the physical environment (calling a halt to pollution, ecological destruction, inner-city decay, etc.) but also the quality of the social and economic institutions which would be seen as determining (and hampering) the chances of the full use and development of human capacities (calling for an end to the degradation of work, and of play; the degradation of culture by the mass media; and the degradation of politics by manipulative oligarchic parties; in short, checking and overcoming the modern phenomena of alienation and domination.)

It is true that even such a society would still need a principle of allocation of the whole social product, as long as the productivity of the society was not sufficient to take care of all the wants of all its members without some principle of rationing, and the rationing principle would most easily be cast in terms of distributive justice. It would be hazardous to predict how long such a rationing principle would be needed. Perhaps a few more decades after such a transformation of society; but not indefinitely, for the need for rationing depends not on productivity alone, or on levels of material desire alone, but on the relation between them. And it seems reasonable to expect that, if we are not taken over by an anti-democratic corporatist state, we can manage a less than infinite level of material desire, and a higher level of productivity.

We may conclude, then, that, if the democratic state survives, other values will have a higher priority than distributive justice. The concept of distributive justice would not be put down, it would wither away.

(ii) Commutative justice

We have still to ask about the prospects of the concept of commutative justice. How substantial is its twentieth-century revival, and will the forces which led to that revival keep it up?

The extent of the revived use of the concept of commutative justice in Western countries' legislation and judicial decisions is at first sight quite impressive. For instance, the US federal 'Uniform Commercial Code', parts of which have been implemented by legislation in some of the American states, permits the courts to refuse to enforce 'unconscionable' contracts or clauses in contracts. The law of contract, which used to be the mainstay of pure market relations, and had no ethical content, is now, in the common-law countries, being reinterpreted to include a minimum ethical content. A notable and influential judicial instance of this in the English courts was Lord Denning's judgement,[12] setting out as a general principle that contracts are voidable if made in conditions of inequality of bargaining power, whether the inequality was due to the weaker party's urgent need or his ignorance or infirmity or inability to get independent advice. Subsequent cases in courts elsewhere have followed a similar pattern. Recent Canadian cases have relieved the weaker party from contracts which embodied both a large inequality of values exchanged and an inequality of bargaining power.[13] The judicial concept of unconscionable contracts seems to incorporate, though it is not based solely on , the commutative principle of exchange of equal values. And some recent legislation has gone so far as to make 'gross excess of price' a ground for non-enforceability of a contract.[14]

So, in political and legal practice, the concept of commutative economic justice appears to have taken on a new life. This may be seen as a new defensive action, of the democratic state on behalf of the little man and the consumer. It is certainly new. In the nineteenth-century highly competitive market model, in which the modern law of contract was developed, the consumer and the little man were thought to be at no disadvantage: their interests were thought to be fully protected by the very fact of the highly competitive nature of the system. But now, when big business has become monopolistic or oligopolistic, the consumer and the little man (and woman) see that they have no such automatic protection and have been able to get the state to intervene on their behalf.

So it appears that the old concept of cummutative justice, which from the seventeenth to nineteenth centuries had succumbed to the dominance of the competitive market (which had made commutative justice meaningless), is now being revived as a defence against a new phenomenon, the oligopolistic market.

We may however have some doubts as to how far this judicial and legislative trend is a significant revival of commutative justice. True, in so far as the trend is to disallow contracts made in conditions of unequal bargaining power, the underlying principle may be reduced to commutative justice simply by adding the presumption that unequal bargaining power leads to exchanges of unequal values. But one must notice

[12] *Lloyds Bank Ltd.* v. *Bundy,* (1974) 3 All ER 757-72.
[13] See S. M. Waddams, *The Law of Contracts* (Canada Law Book Ltd., Toronto, 1977), p. 334, and generally, Ch. 14 on 'Unconscionability'.
[14] *Ibid.,* p. 335.

that disallowance on that ground has not been carried very far. If it had been, the courts would have had to disallow a great many wage contracts—indeed all wage contracts except those made by trade unions that were as powerful as the employing corporations (or state agencies).

A different doubt arises about legislation and judicial decisions which directly use the test of 'exchange of equal values', or condemn contracts embodying 'gross excess of price'. In these cases we must ask what the measure of values, or of excess of price, is. And apparently the measure is simply the supposed price that would have been set by the market if it had been fully competitive. 'Normal' market price is taken as the just price. This is scarcely a revival of the old commutative justice, which tried to control market price by imposing a just price based on traditional social needs. Now, instead, a hypothetical competitive market price is being used to try to control actual uncompetitive market price. Still, it is like the old commutative justice in that it does embody a notion of a just price which is taken to have been the norm in an earlier society: the earlier society, now, is the liberal competitive market society. Legislators and judges who cherish liberal market values are thus quite at home with the new justice in exchange.

But this revival of something like commutative justice is not likely to have any longer a run, in the Western world, than the concept of distributive justice, in the face of the late twentieth-century trend to the state takeover of the allocative market. If corporate capital replaces the democratic state with a corporatist state, electoral expediency will no longer require legislation protecting the weaker bargainer. If, on the contrary, the democratic state flourishes and takes over the control of capital, the justice of private contracts will sink in importance compared with the larger issues of quality of life. Commutative justice, like distributive, will either be put down or wither away.

The only thing that is likely to prolong the life of the concept of economic justice is the growing pressure of the Third World countries which naturally press the concept of economic justice in the hope of improving their position *vis-à-vis* the economically advanced world. The Third World countries are able to put their claims in terms of either distributive or commutative justice. In the terms of world-wide distributive justice, measured either by need or by desert, they can make a strong claim. They can also make a strong claim in terms of commutative justice, since they can easily demonstrate that the capitalist world, by virtue of its superior strength in an oligopolistic international market, imposes unfair terms of trade on them. Thus Third World countries will still find the concept of economic justice a useful offensive or defensive weapon against their economic subjugation by the advanced countries. This will even be reflected back into the conscience of left-liberal circles in the rich countries, but that will scarcely check the erosion of the concept there.

In summary, then, it seems probable that the concept of economic justice will not have a very long future. It will struggle along for some decades yet in the capitalist countries (and longer in the Third World), until in the advanced countries it is either brought down entirely by a totalitarian or corporatist state, or is transcended in a new society by a concept of human fulfilment which will surpass the concept of economic justice.

CHAPTER 2

Problems of Human Rights in the Late Twentieth Century

One might think that everybody must be in favour of human rights. There might be some doubts about animals' rights, and even more doubts about whether trees have rights (a question which has been seriously raised), but surely we might expect that no humans would decry human rights. Yet many of them do, especially since the enlargement of the concept of human rights that was formalized in the United Nations Universal Declaration of Human Rights in 1948.

The only persons who now uniformly endorse human rights are politicians (and they usually do so in terms that are rather noncommital, particularly about the economic and social rights asserted in the UN Declaration). Philosophers and political theorists are divided: some see the new human rights' package as a logically indefensible mess. Businessmen are sceptical or hostile, seeing human rights advocacy as the thin edge of a wedge that is being driven into the historic rights of private enterprise and market freedoms. Lawyers may be divided according to their positions or aspirations: those who are or intend to be corporation lawyers will share the businessman's scepticism or hostility; those who have, or seek, a career in the civil service will model themselves on the politicians' flexible or ambiguous position; those who choose private practice will, being private enterprisers, trim their sails to the prevailing or expected winds.

We should not be surprised at such division of opinion about human rights. For in any class-divided society and, above all, in a class-divided world—I mean a world divided into the poor nations and the rich nations—the slogan 'human rights' is bound to appear—as it has historically been—something of a threat to the established order. That was certainly the case in the French Revolution, when the 'rights of man' were pressed as a weapon against the highly unequal class state of the old regime. And it is so again now, when human rights, now much expanded to include all sorts of economic and social rights, as well as the civil liberties and political rights which were the main demands of the eighteenth-century declarations, promise to be, at least, unsettling to the prevailing social and economic order, both within the capitalist countries and the Communist countries and the Third World countries.

Perhaps the most general reason why the world is still so short of human rights, in spite of the fact that all governments pay at least lip service to them, and sometimes write them into the constitution, is that people don't want human rights as much as they want other things which are, or which they believe are, incompatible with some human rights—colonial liberation, for instance (which may require revolutionary action and incur counter-revolutionary activities, not conducive to civil liberties, pro tem), or rapid economic growth, or what the sociologists call upward social and economic mobility, meaning a system where some people can expect to climb up some rungs on the socio-economic ladder, at the expense of others if necessary.

I want in this chapter to look into some of these problems—some of the reasons why human rights are limping.

Let us get clear, first of all, what we are talking about when we talk about human rights. There is general agreement, both amongst those who want them all and those who have strong reservations about some of them, that the term 'human rights', at least ever since the UN Declaration of 1948, is used to cover three ranges of rights: (1) the civil rights and liberties, i.e. freedom of speech and publication; freedom of association; freedom of religion; freedom of movement within, and out of, and back to, one's country; freedom from arbitrary arrest and imprisonment; and freedom from arbitrary invasion, by governments and other citizens, of personal property; (2) the political right to a voice, directly, or indirectly through the choice of representatives, in the government of the country; and (3) a newer range of what are called economic and social rights, such as the right to work; the right to equal pay for work of equal value; the right to social security against the consequences of illness, old age, death of the breadwinner, and involuntary unemployment; the right to an income consistent with a life of human dignity; the right to rest and leisure (even including the right to holidays with pay); and the right to education. All of these are asserted as rights of *individual* persons, rights that ought to be enjoyed by all individuals equally, with no discrimination on grounds of race, religion, political affiliation, age, or sex.

By contrast, *collective* rights which are claimed by or for subordinate nationalities and subjected native peoples are not generally considered under the head of human rights. They are not in the UN Universal

Declaration of Human Rights. We may wonder why not. The obvious answer is that they raised extremely awkward political problems for many of the member states. The only logical ground that might be offered for leaving out such collective rights is that they are needed, not by individuals universally, but only by certain historically defined groups against others. But that is to overlook the fact that membership in a national or cultural community which has defined itself historically is part of what it means to be human, and is sometimes the most important part. Thus the right to national self-determination may be humanly more important to its claimants than any of the individual rights (as well as being seen as necessary to securing the latter). And the right of a subjected native people to its traditional way of life and to the resources necessary to maintain it may be the greater part of what it means to them to be human (as well as being, in the extreme case where genocide is threatened or is in process, prerequisite to any other rights).

Here is a whole range of problems which twentieth-century framers of charters of rights commonly overlook. In the cause of individual rights they abstract the individual from history: they cut down the individual to the abstract pattern that was appropriate and most needed in the seventeenth and eighteenth centuries, when the big problem was to get the individual free from the many entrenched impediments to the flowering of the human personality. We must soon rethink the dimensions of our cherished individualism, but for the present I shall confine myself to the problems—and there are enough of them—which arise even with the present truncated concept of human rights. I return therefore to the three kinds of rights in the UN Declaration.

A striking feature of these three categories of individual human rights is the differences, both historical and logical, between them. The first two, the civil and political rights, go back to the seventeenth and eighteenth centuries: they were the main objectives of the English and French and American revolutions of those centuries. The third category, the economic and social rights, is much more recent: they began to be talked about by some nineteenth-century socialists, but only become respectable during and after the Second World War. Logically, too, the three categories are different. The civil rights are chiefly rights *against* the state, that is, claims for individual freedoms which the state cannot invade. The political rights are rights to a voice *in the control* of the state. The economic and social rights are claims for benefits to be guaranteed *by* the state, both by legislation and by positive provision of services and income supplements.

No one of the three is necessarily, in all circumstances, incompatible with either or both of the others. In some circumstances they may be mutually reinforcing. But in other circumstances, which all too often prevail, some of them will be, or will appear to be, incompatible with the others. We shall have to look at this more closely in any search for the reasons why human rights have not been implemented any farther than they have. Perhaps we can pin down the circumstances in which they are, or are thought to be, incompatible, and even determine in which circumstances the incompatibility is real and in which it is falsely supposed. That would still leave us with the little problem of changing the world so far as to remove the circumstances in which the incompatibility is real, but it would at least put our problem in perspective.

We can perhaps best come at this by noticing the pretty obvious differences in the extent to which the three types of rights are effectively implemented in different parts of the world today. This has something to do with the century in which the different rights claims emerged in different parts of the world, and even more to do with the economic substructure of the societies in which they emerged. We may use the familiar threefold classification: (1) the Western liberal capitalist world, (2) the Communist world, and (3) the Third World of the under-developed countries. But we shall have to notice that the Third World is itself partly Communist (e.g. China, Vietnam, Cuba), partly capitalist oriented (e.g. most Latin American states), and partly non-Communist but quasi-socialist (e.g. most of the newly independent African states).

About some of the differences in the extent of observance of the three types of rights in these different worlds there is little dispute, at least among Western observers, and one likes to think that their view would be endorsed by an impartial observer from another planet. On civil liberties the developed Communist states are far behind, on the political rights (or effective popular participation) somewhat behind, and on economic and social rights (to work, to social security) somewhat ahead of the Western states. Of the underdeveloped countries, the Communist ones share the position of the developed Communist states, most of the capitalist-oriented ones are badly behind in all three kinds of rights, and the in-between ones have varying records.

Various reasons may be offered for these differences, but it is clear that no single factor is sufficient to explain them. The degree of economic development alone does not do so: some underdeveloped states are better, and some are worse, on some counts than some developed ones. Nor does the type of the economy alone explain the differences in human rights implementation: some states in the capitalist orbit are worse in respect of all human rights, and some are better in respect of some human rights, than the Communist states. It does, however, seem likely that the two factors—the degree of economic development and the type of economy—may in their various combinations account for the differences in implementation and allow us to judge in what circumstances the classic human rights and the newly claimed human rights are inconsistent with each other.

A useful way to come at this is to look at the argument made by some critics of the principles of the UN Declaration of Human Rights, notably the objections of Professor Maurice Cranston. He has argued repeatedly[1] that the inclusion, in the UN Declaration, of economic and social rights (to social security, a decent income, even to holidays with pay) is both philosophically and politically objectionable. I shall not go over all the ground covered in his controversy with Professor Raphael, but I think it is worth drawing attention to something that has gone by default in Cranston's case. He argues that only the traditional human rights—'political and civil rights such as the rights to life, liberty and a fair trial' should be counted as universal human rights, and that the concept of human rights 'has been muddled, obscured and debilitated in recent years by an attempt to incorporate into it specific rights of a different logical category'[2] namely the economic and social rights which are given equal status in the UN Declaration.

There is indeed a sense in which the two sorts of rights are logically different: as we have noticed, the traditional rights are mainly rights of the individual *against* the state, or rights to a preventive say in state policy, whereas the newer economic and social rights are claimed as material benefits (income, social security, leisure) that ought to be provided to all individuals *by* the state. Thus the traditional and the newer rights are held to be not so much inconsistent as logically disparate. When attention is confined, as it is in that argument, to the civil-liberties component of traditional civil rights, the contrast is evident. But when one notices that one of the essential traditional civil rights was, and still is, the right to property, presented as a natural right necessarily required by the right to life or by the right to a free or genuinely human life, the logical disparity between the traditional and

[1] In his *Human Rights Today* (Ampersand, London, 1962); his controversy with Professor D. D. Raphael in essays 4, 5, 8, and 9 in *Political Theory and the Rights of Man*, ed. D. D. Raphael (Macmillan, London, 1967); and his *What are Human Rights?* (Bodley Head, London, 1973).

[2] *What are Human Rights?*, p. 65.

the newer concepts of human rights disappears. They are both then seen for what they are—claims for a right to life at a genuinely human level. All that has changed is the acceptable view of possible ways of securing the individual right to the material means of a fully human life. In the seventeenth and eighteenth centuries it was generally held that it required an individual right to property in land and capital on which one could work to produce the means of life. This was immediately extended (as by Locke) to a right to private appropriation of unlimited amounts, and was later broadened to include freedom of contract (and of bequest) and all the market freedoms, and was extended to include the right of artificial persons (the modern corporation) as well as of natural persons. These extended property rights have become part of the positive law of the Western (and the underdeveloped) capitalist states. Yet the extended property rights are surely as much economic and social rights, to be guaranteed by the state, as any of the newly claimed ones: there is no logical disparity between them.

But while there is no logical disparity between the civil right to property and the newly claimed economic and social rights, there is a real incompatibility between the capitalist property right and the new social and economic rights. Those who are concerned to protect the right of private capital accumulation are quite correct in seeing that that right is threatened by the new social and economic rights claims. Implementation of the new claims in the advanced countries would clearly reduce the rate of capital accumulation there. It is no wonder that Western capital opposes and Western governments are lukewarm about the new claims, and that they welcome any denigration of the UN Declaration: they see that it was pressure from the Third World and the Communist world that put the new rights in the Declaration.

It is unfortunate that Professor Cranston's argument, though he cannot have intended it, gives aid and comfort to those Western governments who are dragging their feet about human rights. His charge of logical disparity, though unfounded, is plausible enough to distract attention from the real opposition of interests: if his view were to be widely accepted in the West, the sluggishness in the legal implementation of human rights there would be encouraged by its real source being concealed.

Thus the position of human rights, at least of the new ones, in the West seems to be due to the type of economic system. The capitalist economy necessarily works against the new human rights, while the capitalist concept of property, treating it as a natural individual (and corporate) right rather than a social right, lends plausibility to the claim that the new social and economic rights are logically disparate from, and have less standing than, the older rights.

What of the Communist and Third World countries, who have pushed the new claims to the neglect of the traditional ones? Is their stand to be explained in terms of their departure from the Western economic system, or by their degree of economic development, or both?

Let us look first at the Third World, where the degree of economic development is the most evident factor. Some of those countries, of course, notably in Latin America, have been kept thoroughly within the Western economic system by ruling groups whose whole position depends on pleasing foreign capital and keeping the country under-developed or misdeveloped: there, there are neither any civil liberties nor much in the way of economic and social rights. But in other Third World countries, those which have departed significantly from the Western system and whose governments are genuinely trying to avoid or break away from neo-colonial subjection to foreign capital, there are also obstacles to human rights. There, the rulers' perception of their countries' ills as all due to economic underdevelopment easily leads them to subordinate human rights to economic growth.

They are encouraged in this by the case that can be made, and often is made in the West, in terms of a 'trade-off'. The notion of a trade-off is perhaps most familiar in economics but is readily extended to many kinds of decision-making. Individuals, and whole societies, in so far as they act by rational calculation, are continually having to decide, as between two things they value, how much of one they are willing to do without in order to get some amount of the other. This is what is meant by a 'trade-off'. How much leisure time will an individual exchange ('trade-off') for how much income? How much clean air will a whole community do without for the sake of the convenience of the private automobile, or how much air and water pollution will it put up with for the benefit of cheaper paper, steel, or manufactured goods? Such choices are most required in affluent consumer-oriented societies, but similar questions are posed in any society which has glimpsed a more plentiful future.

Now the sort of trade-offs just mentioned seem morally neutral, or even morally laudable: the individual or the community is making a free choice between two goods according to his/her/its own evaluation. Some moralists, indeed, would have strong reservations about trading off certain civil rights for any utilitarian benefits, and most would insist at least that in any trade-off calculation, the costs and benefits to future generations should be taken into account. But however we may differ on such points, we can surely all agree that a trade-off is unjustifiable if one set of people get the benefits and a different set of people bear the costs.

Now let us apply this to the case that is often made for some trade-off between human rights and economic development in the underdeveloped countries. The argument is that to achieve a level of productivity that could provide a decently human life for everyone in that country, a measure of economic development is required which is only possible with some temporary sacrifice of civil and/or political rights, for instance the right of association in free trade unions, the right to strike, even freedom of speech and publication.

In the case of a country in which the material level is so low that a decent human subsistence for everyone cannot presently be provided, the case for a trade-off is attractive. It needs only a demonstration (a) that the sacrifice of some human rights was necessary for, and *would* lead to, the requisite economic growth, and (b) that the resulting increase in the national output *would* be fully applied to the enhancement of the human condition of all the members of the society.

As to (a), there are certainly dictatorships in the third world (e.g. Taiwan) where great economic growth has accompanied the denial of civil rights, and we may reasonably suppose that the actual growth would not have been achieved without the denial of rights. Although this does not demonstrate that an adequate growth *necessarily* requires a denial of civil and political rights, it does set up a presumption that in some circumstances that denial will bring about an otherwise unlikely economic growth.

It is with respect to (b) that the trade-off case generally collapses. The rulers of most of the underdeveloped states (certainly of the capitalist-oriented ones) who have used the trade-off argument to justify their denial of civil and political rights, have not used any increased material productivity which might be attributed to that denial for improving the lot of their own poor: the suppression of trade unions, of political parties, and of elementary civil liberties, has usually benefited only a small ruling group: one need think only of the current Latin American dictatorial regimes.

The denial of civil and political rights does indeed favour capital accumulation in the hands of an economic élite, but they are as apt to put it in Swiss banking accounts as to reinvest it at home; and even where they do invest it at home, it is usually in capital-intensive projects, rather than the labour-intensive projects which are usually more appropriate to the economic development of the poorest countries, and which would raise the standard of living of their poor. Again, the denial of civil and political rights by a ruling junta is undoubtedly an encouragement to foreign investment in an underdeveloped country; but since the purpose of foreign investors must be to keep the recipient country in dependence on them, foreign investment is not conducive to civil and political rights which interfere with that dependence. Nor is it likely to bring any improvement in economic and social rights, since they also are apt to reduce the rate of return to foreign investors. In all such cases we may indeed say there has been a trade-off: civil rights have been traded for rapid economic growth. But it cannot be morally justified even on utilitarian grounds, for it is the people's rights that have been traded for the rulers' benefits.

In non-dictatorial regimes where the ruling party is genuinely devoted to enhancing the human condition, but thinks it necessary to resort to some trade-off of rights for economic growth, the benefits to the people are also likely to be illusory. Any reduction of civil rights in the interests of economic development is all too apt to be taken farther than is necessary to provide a material standard adequate for a decent human life for all. 'Modernization' comes to be put first. Economic growth itself becomes a fetish. The ruling party in newly independent states, however much it rejected the capitalist ethos, is insensibly caught up in the central capitalist article of faith, the worship of economic growth. I am not suggesting that economic growth is undesirable as such: it may well be a necessary means to a human level of subsistence for all in an underdeveloped country. But there are twin dangers in such a country bending its efforts to economic growth: both dangers arise from the fact that the concept of economic growth—both its purpose and its practice—comes from the ideology and the experience of capitalist society.

As to the ideology, economic growth is so essential to capitalism that the directors of capitalist societies come to take it as an end in itself, to which everything else may appropriately be subordinated. The government of an underdeveloped country, in taking over the concept of economic growth, is very likely to absorb also the ideology that goes with it, to make economic growth an end instead of a means, an end which is then taken to justify otherwise unjustifiable means.

As to practice, the same underdeveloped government is apt also to take over some of the capitalist techniques which once brought such spectacular economic growth in the West, even though they no longer do so there: notably, investment in capital-intensive enterprises and advanced technologies, which in capitalism are judged successful to the extent that they lead to still more capital accumulation. The danger here is not from the use of improved technology as such: the whole world must increasingly rely on advancing technology to release humankind from scarcity. The danger is simply that the capitalist criterion for its successful use will be accepted. Where the criterion is accumulation, human rights haven't much chance.

The weaknesses of the trade-off case are obvious enough. The frightening thing is that the trade-off argument is nevertheless politically very attractive to the rulers of underdeveloped countries.

What we must now notice is that the trade-off argument is also attractive to the rulers of the Communist countries, even of the most economically advanced ones, engaged as they are in strenuous military and civilian competition with the West. As long as they give top priority to catching up with, or surpassing, Western rates of productivity, they have a strong incentive to withhold the civil and political liberties which would inhibit that development.

Thus in the Third World and the Communist world there are powerful forces against the civil and political rights, forces which are attributable in both cases to the relative economic underdevelopment of those countries. Their rulers may pride themselves on having implemented, although at a low level, some of the new rights such as the right to work and to social security. One may even suspect that it is because their record on civil and political rights is bad that they play up their concern for social and economic rights: it makes them look good in the world forum of public opinion. But whether the concern of those governments for social and economic rights is genuine or contrived, it does not justify the denial of civil and political rights, for without the civil and political rights the citizens can have no assurance that their economic and social rights will have much substance. Any such trade-off is convenient for the rulers but illusory for the citizens.

If this were a problem only in the Communist and Third Worlds it would be bad enough, but it goes farther than that: it penetrates into the first world as well. What has rarely been noticed but must no longer be overlooked is the strong probability that Western governments will resort to a similar trade-off argument in the name of their countries' sustained economic growth. Such a disposition is already foreshadowed in the talk about the 'ungovernability' of Western democracies put out by the high-level Trilateral Commission. Western governments' resort to a trade-off of civil and political rights is probable because the rate of economic growth, on which the whole structure of civil and political rights in our societies has depended, is rapidly declining. Business and government leaders have only recently begun to recognize that decline, though without entertaining the idea that it might be the result of a structural defect of the system. The remedies they propose are belt-tightening by the rank and file. To put that across they must at least resist all popular pressures for a more effective democratic input into government decisions, that is, they must hold down or reduce effective political rights. And that can easily lead to a tighter rein on civil liberties as well. In effect, the decline in the rate of economic growth in the capitalist countries is putting their rulers in the same boat as the rulers of the underdeveloped countries and the communist countries. To the rulers in the West, the slowing down of capitalist growth *is* underdevelopment in relation to their expectations, and it would be surprising if they did not take up similar trade-off arguments at the expense of political and civil rights.

Are any ways forward to be gleaned from all this? The first lesson to be drawn from any such analysis is that human rights are, in fact and in prospect, subordinate. They necessarily take second place to the desires of peoples or rulers for other things: for national self-determination, for a place in the sun, for military security, for hegemony, for the mainten-ance of inequality within nations and (of which we are all guilty) inequality between rich and poor nations. Human rights are caught up in these more pressing concerns. Thus, so long as the Cold War, now warmer, now colder, persists, the prospects for civil and political rights in the Communist countries are slight, and the maintenance of such of those rights as are still enjoyed in capitalist countries is at risk. Similarly, so long as the rich nations persist in policies which widen the gap between them and the poor nations, there is not much hope of an improvement in civil and political rights in the poor nations.

Does this mean, then, that devotees of human rights should give up? That they should stop talking about human rights, and concentrate instead on the issues which seem to determine the prospects of human rights? Should they drop human rights, and go all out for *détente*, dis-armament, and genuine aid to the Third World? Vital as these latter are, I do not think that we should drop the human rights case.

For the second lesson is that the demand for human rights is itself one of the forces already working to put inequality, and war-oriented governments, and the worship of economic growth, on the defensive. It makes a more direct demand on the conscience of liberals in the affluent Western societies than anything else can do, and in those societies that conscience is not yet entirely negligible. And the conscientious Western liberal is, along with the conscientious democratic socialist, now the main resource against the manifold injustices of today's world, and hence against the confrontational posture of West vs. East, and North vs. South. The conscientious Communist hasn't much chance in his homeland, as long as his leaders can point to the Cold War. And in most of the Third World the educational level is so low that no voices except those of the educated élite are heard, and their concern for human rights is tragically related to what they see as the imperative of rapid economic development.

What is needed, to give added force to the liberal conscience, and perhaps also the Third World forces for human rights, is a clearer view of necessary and possible relations between human rights and the world forces that dominate them. We should not stop pressing for human rights, but in pressing for them we should be aware how much they are at the mercy of other widely held values, and should consider what changes in those values are required. I have suggested so far that the villain is the worship of economic growth. Certainly we need to rethink the priority we have given it, since it puts the strongest strain on human rights in all three worlds. If the actual rate of economic growth in the West continues to decline towards zero, we in the West will have to abandon that priority, which will open up the way for a new concern for human rights.

But more than that is needed. We shall also have to rethink the role of the property right. It used to be thought obvious that a virtually unlimited property right was one of the essential human rights. Some still think it so, but many liberals (as well as the socialists) now think the opposite—their slogan is 'Human rights, not property rights!' The world seems to be divided into proponents of the one or the other. I have suggested elsewhere[3] that a way out of this apparent impasse might be found by treating all the human rights as individual property rights. My point was simply that the property right is so deeply embedded in the Western liberal tradition that we might more effectively campaign for human rights by treating them as individual property rights than by treating human and property rights as opposites. To do that requires no sleight of hand. To speak of human rights as individual property rights would indeed be to restore the original liberal meaning of property, as

---

[3] 'Human Rights as Property Rights', Ch. 6, below.

when Locke and his contemporaries spoke of a property in one's person, one's life and liberty, as well as one's worldly goods.

To move the liberal concept of property ahead again in this way would certainly not solve all our problems. It would be at most a short-term remedy to our faulty time-bound thinking, for our thinking still retains the early liberal notion of the individual as a being prior to and rightfully independent of society or community. In the longer run we shall need a more realistic concept of what it is to be human. We shall need to recognize that the individual can be fully human only as a member of a community.

Paradoxically, that recognition now seems more likely to be generated within the Western countries than in the Third World. Paradoxically, because one would expect that the priority of community would be a more natural assumption in the Third World countries, which are closer to the pre-capitalist idea that one's humanity was more a matter of one's membership in the community than of one's freedom from the community, that the greatest human right was the right of belonging to the community, and the severest deprivation was to be cast out. But what has happened is that the Third World countries, in so far as they are struggling against their previous subservience to the West, have had to use Western ideological weapons. They have had to base their claims, in the world forum, on their need to promote the modernization which would permit the enhancement of the individual. Aboriginal people threatened with submergence within First World countries do still invoke community values, but the Third World has largely given in to the Western values. Their search for rapid economic development has put them under strong pressure to abandon community values.

Given that the Third World has fallen into a worship of economic growth taken over from the West, and that this endangers human rights in the Third World even more immediately than it does in the West, is there any hope for human rights world-wide? On my analysis, the prospects are not good anywhere. As I have argued, in the Communist countries, and the Third World countries outside the capitalist-oriented ones, there are strong inherent forces against civil and political rights, though nothing in principle against social and economic rights (since those countries have abandoned the capitalist property right). In the capitalist-oriented Third World countries there are strong inherent forces against both kinds of human rights. And in the advanced Western capitalist countries there are inherent forces against the social and economic rights (because they are impediments to corporate capital accumulation), and an increasing probability that effective political rights and civil liberties will be reduced because they would impede their governments' attempts to cope with the slow-down of advanced capitalist economies to a no-growth condition.

On this analysis there is only one ray of hope for the future of human rights. That is that we in the West may realize before it is too late that the expectation of our sustained economic growth is a delusion; that we must settle for something much less; and that the Third World, which has followed our follies up till now, may follow our belated wisdom in giving up that mirage.

CHAPTER 3

The Prospects of Economic and Industrial Democracy

Demands for what are called economic and industrial democracy are heard increasingly in both the capitalist and socialist worlds. And in some countries in each world a significant amount of workers' participation in industrial decision-making has already been achieved. What are the future prospects? This is a question which increasingly concerns labour and capitalist and socialist governments and enterprises. I propose, as a political theorist, to consider chiefly the *political* factors that may be expected to influence or determine the prospects of economic and industrial democracy in the foreseeable future.

1. Definitions

Neither economic nor industrial democracy is at all clearly defined in ordinary usage.

Economic democracy is the less clearly defined, but it is generally used to mean an arrangement of the economic system which will give a just distribution of work, income and wealth in a country. One might question whether this should be called democracy at all, even by analogy. For the defining characteristic seems to be the existence of distributive justice rather than a mechanism of control, whereas democracy, whatever else it means, means at least a mechanism of control.

However, economic democracy can reasonably be called a kind of democracy on two grounds. First, it clings to a well-established meaning of democracy as not merely a system of government controlled by or responsible to the people, but as a kind of society where all persons have equal effective right to a fully human life. Such a society clearly requires a just distribution of work and income. So it may properly be said that the just distribution is demanded not as an end in itself but as a means to a democratic society. As such, the demand may be called a demand for democracy.

Secondly, and conversely, one may reasonably assume that a just distribution of work and income requires a substantial measure of democratic *political* control, or direction, of the economy. That may range from a fully socialist control of the allocation of economic resources, to a greater or lesser measure of intervention by a democratic state in a capitalist economy. In any case, if the assumption is granted, a demand for a just distribution of economic goods is a demand for an effective political democracy.

Industrial democracy is more directly about control: indeed, the term is sometimes used as synonymous with 'workers control'. Most broadly, it means an organization of a productive unit whereby all those working in it have an effective voice in decisions affecting their work. The unit may be anything from the shop-floor level to the level of the plant, the enterprise, or the whole industry.

Industrial democracy is logically distinct from economic democracy in two ways. First, industrial democracy is primarily concerned with decisions about *production* (about conditions of work, methods of production, and even goals and allocation of production), whereas economic democracy is primarily about the distribution of social goods throughout the whole society. Secondly, in so far as industrial democracy has a secondary concern with distribution (i.e. the sharing of rewards for work), it need not seek the goals of economic democracy; for instance, an enterprise with strong workers' control might keep all the surplus earnings of the enterprise for its own members rather than sharing them with members of other enterprises as would be required in principle by economic democracy.

Nevertheless, industrial democracy at the broadest level merges into economic democracy. Where industrial democracy is making decisions about the goals and allocation of production in a whole industry, those decisions will necessarily affect and be affected by overall national economic policy, which is necessarily concerned with distribution as well as production: here, industrial democracy must come to terms with economic democracy (and with political democracy as well). There is a close connection in the other direction also. Economic democracy is about the just distribution not only of the GNP — the material output of the whole society — but also the just distribution of other social goods, including the possibility of engaging in meaningful work. Thus one of the goals of economic democracy is the same as the goal of industrial democracy.

In this chapter I shall give most attention to industrial democracy, partly because it is a little more precise than economic democracy, and partly because I think that demands for industrial democracy are likely, at least in capitalist countries, to be a main propellant towards economic democracy, rather than the other way around. The proviso 'at least in capitalist countries' points to another distinction that requires some attention.

2. Capitalist and Socialist Societies

Without getting into the vexed question of whether today's socialist countries are state capitalisms, it seems reasonable to assume that there are significant differences between the capitalist and socialist worlds with respect to the prospects of industrial democracy. Conditions conducive to and hostile to an increase of industrial democracy are at first sight quite different in the two worlds. In capitalism, the imperative of unlimited private capital accumulation is dominant, in socialism it is not. Again, in a capitalist economy there is necessarily a conflict of interest between capital and labour; in a socialist economy, that conflict is not necessary. Yet that conflict will be present in a socialist economy in which the government thinks its highest priority is to catch up to the productivity of the most advanced capitalist economies. There it will take the form of a conflict of interest between, on the one hand, a central state apparatus which, intent on achieving a high rate of capital accumulation, adopts capitalist methods of maximizing the efficiency of labour—one thinks of Lenin's acceptance of Taylorism, and on the other hand, a labour force which resists Taylorism as contradictory to human work needs. Thus as long as a socialist state gives priority to catching up to capitalist productivity, the forces for and against industrial democracy in that state will be much the same as in an advanced capitalist state. Indeed, as I shall suggest, the prospects of industrial democracy in such a socialist state may be worse than in a capitalist state. For as we shall see, in advanced capitalism the state may have to step in to require or guarantee some industrial democracy, whereas in a socialist society intent on catching up it will be precisely the state which will be apt to oppose or prevent any measure of workers' control which is deemed incompatible with industrial efficiency and high productivity.

But that is to take us ahead of our analysis. The only point I want to make here is that in socialist countries which give a high priority to approaching or catching up with capitalist productivity (that is to say, almost all the socialist countries), the position of industrial democracy is not necessarily very different from its position in capitalist countries.

It is evident, too, that in both socialist and capitalist societies, economic questions are political ones: economic relations have become inextricably interwoven with the political system. In capitalism, the state is increasingly pulled into the economy: to support it, to regulate it, sometimes to save it from itself, sometimes to save human beings from it. And of course in socialism the state is expected to dominate the economy and to control it even more closely.

Moreover, in so far as the state (capitalist or socialist) is democratic it will respond roughly to economic demands made on it from several directions: from particular capitals and/or various levels of the state and party apparatus, from trade unions and other organizations of producers, and from citizens as consumers. Political pressures from labour and consumers will depend on their level of consciousness about needs and wants, about the relative merits of the consumer society and the conserver society.

We can expect that the forces for and against industrial democracy will be complex. And they will be changing as the relations between state and economy change. We may hope that a look at this from the political angle may be rewarding, though all we can do is to list, and relate to each other, without trying to measure for any one country, the forces for and against. Even this cannot be done thoroughly in a brief chapter, but a beginning can be made. I shall start by considering the forces for and against *industrial* democracy in *capitalist* countries. I shall speak of the forces for and against an *increase* in the present amount of industrial democracy in those countries, abstracting from national differences in the present amount. On this I shall offer six hypotheses and say just enough about each to suggest what empirical studies would be needed to validate or invalidate them.

It will not be difficult then to see how well they apply also to socialist countries.

3. Hypotheses re Determinants of Industrial Democracy in Capitalist Countries

(a) The demand for industrial democracy will increase in the measure that the capitalist economy, however much managed by the state, is seen to have become incompetent to provide the economic goods which it has led the working class to expect.

(b) The demand will be resisted by capital in the measure that particular capitals understand their own interests.

(c) Working-class *industrial* action will be supplemented or supplanted by working-class *political* action in the measure that the rate of unemployment increases.

(d) Pressure for industrial democracy will *require* working-class *political* action in the measure that a capitalist economy is unable to fulfil the expectations it has engendered.

(e) Industrial democracy will not get very far unless the state fosters it.

(f) The state will only foster it in so far as the state has got relative autonomy from particular capitals and is effectively constrained from destroying political democracy.

Let us look at these six propositions in turn.

Proposition (a) relates increase in the demand for industrial democracy to a visible decline in the competence of capitalism to sustain the level of material benefits expected by the working class. The reasoning behind the proposition is quite simple. The record shows that as long as capitalism is prosperous, organized labour can extract concessions in wage and fringe benefits from employers, and will devote its energies largely to that. Reward for work is more important, or at least more readily attainable, than control of work. Consumer gratifications make up for work subservience. But when the economy runs persistently into trouble, business unionism is not enough. Survey research data indicate that, in the abstract, workers value job satisfaction ahead of good wages and other material benefits: this is consistent with their reliance on business unionism in properous times since then it is easier to win wage concessions than to win a voice in the control of work. But when capital cannot afford to provide consumer gratifications, it can expect trouble in maintaining work subservience. There will be increased workers' demand for a voice in the control of work, which is the beginning of an assault on capitalist relations of production.

Proposition (b) asserts that this demand will be resisted by capital in so far as particular capitals understand their own interests. This is fairly evident. The interest of every particular capital (i.e. of each capitalist firm) is to accumulate more capital. Essential to this is the maintenance or improvement of the rate of productivity per man-hour of employed labour. Vital to that is management's control of production methods and production policy. Particular capitals, in so far as they understand this, will hold on to their control of work at almost any cost; and if the cost is merely higher wages, that can easily be afforded by the trend-setting giant corporations who can pass the cost on to the consumer. Moreover, an intelligent capitalist management will see that the demand for workers' control is more dangerous, because less divisive, than any demand for higher wages. Wage demands can be used by capital to turn sections of the working class against each other—skilled vs. unskilled, male vs. female, white vs. black, etc. Demands for workers' control are not so divisive and hence are more dangerous to capital.

Proposition (c) asserts that working-class *industrial* action will give way to working class *political* action in proportion as the level of unemployment increases. The simple point here is that a high level of unemployment inhibits working-class industrial action. Strikes are more difficult. Those who have jobs put job security ahead of wages and work conditions; those out of work have no industrial leverage. But both the employed and the unemployed can have some political leverage, either through labour and social-democratic parties or through trade-union lobbying of non-labour governments. And whether a high level of unemployment is due to deliberate government policy or to the structural incompetence of advanced capitalism, it will be seen to require political action. A persistent high level of unemployment may be taken as evidence of structural incompetence of capitalism. Thus the incompetence which turns workers to political action is the very thing which, according to Proposition (a), turns them from mere business unionism to demanding some industrial democracy.

Proposition (d) simply emphasizes that working-class pressure for industrial democracy, as for any other working-class goals, must take the form of *political* action in the measure that a capitalist economy becomes incompetent. Proposition (d), we might say, is the general rule, of which Proposition (c) is a special case.

Proposition (e), that industrial democracy will not get very far unless the state fosters it, is almost self–evident, given the resistance by capital as set out in Proposition (b) and the insufficiency of merely industrial action as set out in Propositions (c) and (d). Nothing but state action, propelled by working-class political action, is likely to prevail against that resistance. And even where, in the interests of industrial peace, the resistance of capital is lowered, the amount of industrial democracy any firm can afford depends partly on the state's fiscal and economic policies.

Proposition (f) relates the prospects of industrial democracy in capitalist countries to the relative autonomy of the state from particular capitals, and to the concern of a liberal-democratic capitalist state for maintaining its legitimacy. If the state were entirely controlled by corporate capitals, one could not expect it to foster any measure of workers' control. But in advanced capitalist societies the state, while committed to supporting capitalism, has attained a relative autonomy from particular capitals, that is, from particular corporations, groups of corporations, and even whole industries: they have in one way or another become so dependent on the state that the state has some hold over them. Moreover, to serve the interests of capital as a whole, that is, to provide the conditions for continued capital accumulation, the state must frequently disregard or oppose the demands of particular capitals. And it seems likely that the state, in the interests of capital in general, will increasingly have to sponsor measures of industrial democracy in various sectors of the economy in order to get the co-operation of organized labour in such policies as wage restraint and strike restraint, a co-operation which the capitalist state needs increasingly as the economy runs into serious and persistent problems (inflation, unemployment, stagnation or declining growth rate, etc.). All this, of course, depends on the state remaining democratic. If the democratic constitution were overturned, or undermined by plebiscitarian devices, the state would no longer need to ask for co-operation. And if the state then retained any relative autonomy from capital, that autonomy would not likely be used to promote industrial democracy.

If we now look at the combined effect of our six propositions, there appears to be a common factor in all the forces for and against an increase of industrial democracy: they all depend, directly or indirectly, on the probability of the increasing incompetence of capitalism. That is what (by Proposition (a)) raises the demand for industrial democracy. That is what (by (c) and (d)) turns the demand into political channels. That is what (by (f)) gives the state its relative autonomy. And that is what (also by (f)) could lead to the destruction of political and hence industrial democracy.

I know no way of estimating the present relative strength of the forces for and against industrial democracy in any or all capitalist countries. Only one thing emerges clearly—the prospects of industrial democracy there depend largely on the workers' awareness of the dynamics of capitalism, and (consequently) on their changing their priorities from consumer satisfaction to work gratification.

4. Differential Prospects in Socialist Countries

We may now inquire how different or how similar are the forces for and against industrial democracy in socialist countries. Without trying to test the applicability of each of our six propositions to socialist countries, we may observe that the differences between the relevant forces in the two kinds of countries are not as great as one might expect.

It is true that in principle there is no necessary conflict of interests between capital and labour in a socialist society, but there may be a parallel conflict of interest between a central state apparatus which requires a high level of capital accumulation and the wants of the workers, both as consumers and as producers. As consumers they may find any significant improvement in their material standards repeatedly postponed, in the interests of future productivity, by the state giving priority to capital-goods industries; as workers they may find themselves subjected to the same Taylorism, scientific management, and degradation of work, as in capitalist society. Thus there may be a conflict not only between their short-run and long-run interests as consumers, but also between their need for human, unalienated work and the system's need to harness them to technological imperatives.

The victimization of the workers in both these respects can be expected to persist as long as the governments of socialist countries give top priority to catching up with the productivity of advanced capitalist countries. Unfortunately, it is not easy to see an end to the drive to catch up, for it is partly dependent on the arms race. This is a striking illustration of the interdependence of economic and political forces: the chances of economic and industrial democracy depend partly on the politics of disarmament, Cold War, and *détente*, which in turn depend on global contests for economic predominance.

As long as the socialist drive to catch up is given top priority, the chances of industrial democracy seem worse in socialist than in capitalist countries. For, as mentioned earlier, the capitalist state may have to intervene to impose some measure of workers' control on private capital; but in a socialist state which is intent on catching up, it will be precisely the state which will oppose workers' control as being incompatible with the state's ability to maximize productive efficiency.

In the measure that socialist countries do catch up, of course, the pressure to catch up will diminish, and so will that obstacle to industrial democracy. But even before then, the forces making for industrial democracy in socialist countries may gain at the expense of the forces against it. The risky confrontation between the trade-union organization and the state in Poland in 1980-1 shows that organized labour there prizes trade-union independence from the state very highly, and an initial demand for a shorter work week may readily move on to a demand for industrial democracy of varying degrees. The same forces may be assumed to be present, though latent, in the other socialist countries. To the extent that those forces operate, the socialist catch-up state will have to drop or reduce its opposition to industrial democracy. It will have to do so for much the same reason that the state in an incompetent capitalist economy must do so—to avoid being overthrown in a legitimation crisis.

In the face of that imperative, the prospects of industrial democracy in capitalist and socialist countries are not far different. I said before that the prospects in capitalist societies depend largely on the workers' awareness of the dynamics of capitalism, and (consequently) on their changing their priorities from consumer satisfaction to work gratification. In present-day socialist societies, too, the prospects depend on the workers' awareness of the dynamics of capitalism (since that determines the dynamics of catch-up socialism), but there no immediate change is needed in the people's priorities, since the demands for consumer satisfaction and for work gratification will both lead to a relative autonomy of organized labour from the state, and thus to the possibility of an increase in industrial democracy.

CHAPTER 4

Liberalism as Trade-offs

'Trade-off' is a fairly recent addition to the English language but it is now in common use in business and labour circles and by economists, politicians, and political commentators. Negotiators of collective-bargaining agreements speak of trade-offs between wage increases and improved fringe benefits. Corporate spokesmen urge trade-offs of environmental pollution against the higher costs of paper or steel which pollution controls would bring. The public is asked to trade off the dangers of nuclear-energy development against the supposed need for increased sources of energy. Governments are still apt to think in terms of a trade-off between high unemployment and a high rate of inflation, unable to admit that these are no longer alternatives.

To such questions of national economic policy may be added international questions. How much of your imperial suzerainty should you trade off for commercially advantageous wheat sales or exports of machine tools and technologies to countries your foreign office regards as potential enemies? How much of our desire to assist in multilateral disarmament should we trade off for the benefits, in employment and national revenue, of a thriving armaments export industry?

Similar policy decisions are constantly needed at the municipal level: city politicians have repeatedly to think of trade-offs between neighbourhood amenities endangered by property developers and the enhanced assessments and tax revenue expected from the developer's projects.

Other questions arise at the level of purely political mechanics: in determining the best size for semi-autonomous municipal or regional authorities, how much democratic responsiveness should be traded for how much administrative efficiency? And how much responsiveness vs. how much efficiency, in such matters as the structure and role of committees, and the rules of procedure, in Congress or Parliament?

At a different level, many purely individual decisions can be seen as trade-off calculations. How much income shall one forgo for how much leisure, or vice versa? How much cultivating one's garden for how much political activism (a question which has rightly been treated as central by democratic theorists of various persuasions)? How much effort, by industrial or political action, to make one's life in one's workplace more humanly acceptable, as against the consumer income to be expected by accepting the prevailing management-labour relationship? These are questions not far below the surface of most working people's lives in any industrialized society. They may all not unreasonably be called trade-offs.

From these examples a definition of the trade-off is readily collected. It is a decision, or an action resulting from a decision, by an individual or a collectivity (a national or lesser legislature or executive, or a corporation or a trade union) as between two things both of which are desired (positively or negatively) but which are seen, or believed, to be after a certain point incompatible with each other. If the two desires are indeed incompatible alternatives, a choice must be made: so much of one against so much of the other. That is the essence of the trade-off.

The trade-off is now quite generally treated as if it was in the very nature of things. It is certainly an attractive formulation: it appears to put complicated issues into a clear-cut manageable shape. But it is not in the nature of things. For by definition it constricts the choice to two alternatives—so much of (a) as against so much of (b), with no room for a (c) which would obviate the need for choosing between (a) and (b). In other words, it neglects the possibility that a third option, transcending the need for the two-way choice, might be opened up. Yet that possibility is in many cases not inconceivable. An obvious case is the choice between unemployment and inflation, if only because they can already be seen to have become non-alternatives. Again, the choice between arms reduction and maintaining the present level of employment might be obviated by a recognition that the arms industry is less labour-intensive than others to which its share of the labour force might be switched by a shift in national expenditures. Again, the choice between efficiency and democratic responsiveness in the organization of Congress or Parliament depends largely on whose idea of efficiency is accepted.

In all such cases the need for the stipulated trade-off is highly questionable. But this is often not seen. Indeed, for a social issue to be treated as a trade-off, everyone concerned must be overlooking the possibility that a third option might be opened up. That a possible third option has not been conceived may be because it has simply been overlooked, or because it has been kept out of sight by those who have an interest in doing so. And of two contending parties it is of course the stronger which is able to cover up, and the weaker which simply over-looks third possibilities.

So much for the nature of the trade-off.

You may wonder what all this has to do with liberalism. It is not enough to say that the essence of liberalism is choice. We shall be far-ther ahead if we observe that the concept of the trade-off is peculiarly appropriate to liberalism because that concept, like traditional liberalism, assumes that the basic element of society is the rational, maximizing, atomic individual. That, certainly, was the hallmark of liberalism in its eighteenth- and nineteenth-century form—the liberalism of Adam Smith and Bentham. And as I have argued elsewhere, that strain of liberalism was carried on into the liberal–democratic tradition in the twentieth century, in spite of attempts by J. S. Mill and his followers to get away from it. The liberal–democratic theory, and practice, were, we may say, infected by trade-off thinking long before the word was invented.

The question now is whether liberal democracy can transcend that kind of thinking. It is an urgent question if, as I think, the future of liberal democracy, indeed whether liberal democracy has a future, depends on its transcending its trade-off assumptions.

Let us look at the record in liberal theory. The earliest liberals in the Anglo-American tradition were, in my view, the theorists and activists of the English Civil War and Commonwealth periods, ranging from the Levellers to Cromwell and Milton and other republicans, many of whose principles were carried over into American thinking. They started indeed from the rational atomic individual but not from the material-maximizing cost/benefit calculator: they had some notion of higher values. The human essence was the free enjoyment and develop-ment of one's God-given innate nature, and this required freedom of conscience, freedom from arbitrary arrest and imprisonment, freedom of the press and other civil liberties, as well as a secure right to indivi-dual property in material goods. Life and liberty were natural rights, property was either a natural right (as with the Levellers, and later with Locke) or was absolutely indispensable as a fundamental constitutional right (as with Cromwell and Ireton). About political rights, notably the right to choose the representatives who would comprise the legislative bodies, there was less unanimity. But all the theorists of the Civil War and Commonwealth periods (at least those on the non-royalist side) saw the individual, not as essentially a material maximizer or acquisitor, but a creature endowed with a higher nature: it was that higher nature that required certain rights. This was at least one current of seventeenth-century liberal theory, competing with Locke's possessive individualism.[1] It was never fully implemented in practice. The Whig Revolution did something to reduce arbitrary power, but not much to enshrine that earlier developmental liberal vision. That liberalism retreated somewhat in the Whig era but it stayed alive: it resurfaced repeatedly in the eighteenth century (Wilkes, Priestley, Price, and Paine, and the American Declaration of Independence). Human rights still had some standing.

In the nineteenth century all this changed, both in theory and in practice. Benthamism superseded natural rights theories. And in practice, legislatures and courts subordinated human rights to the forseen benefits of giving full rein to the capitalist market economy. Human rights were traded off for economic growth. This was the liberalism of *laissez-faire*. One can see it as early as Hume and Adam Smith who, as noted above, were still able to see man as at the same time both an exerter of innate human capacities and a material maximizer, the latter view enabling them to build on aggregate utility rather than individual natural right.

But by the late nineteenth century in liberal theory, and by the twentieth century in liberal practice, that position had become untenable. Unalloyed capitalism became too grossly incompatible with human dignity. John Stuart Mill and his followers registered this in liberal theory, not before a rising tide of working-class demands had compelled some attention to the claims of the lower orders. And in the twentieth century, when the liberal state had perforce become the liberal-democratic state, these demands resulted in the now familiar welfare state, with its transfer payments designed to put a floor under the incomes of the poor (or, as we now call them, with typical bourgeois delicacy, those on the lower rungs of the socio-economic ladder). The emergence of the liberal welfare state may thus be seen as something of

[1] Kramnick has pointed out that even Locke's individualism was sometimes in the eighteenth century seen as developmental rather than possessive, in that many liberals in England and America cited or quoted or paraphrased Locke as their authority for basing their cases on natural rights and for deducing the right of revolution against governments which denied freedom of conscience or the political freedom of the vote (Issac Kramnick, 'Republican Revisionism Revisited', *American Historical Review*, June 1982). We may observe, however, that in that earliest century of liberalism, from Locke to Adam Smith, developmental and possessive individualism were not yet fully inconsistent: it was the liberalism of a new class, a middling bourgeoisie, who needed to assert the values of possessive individualism to promote their own development at the expense of the old Whig *grande bourgeoisie*.

a reversal in the trade-off pattern: a marginal trade-off of the imperatives of capitalist expansion for a supportable level of human rights. But we must notice that it was only marginal, for the welfare state still relies on capitalist enterprise to provide the wherewithal for the transfer payments. And indeed it is doubtful if the flowering of the welfare state from the 1930s on should be considered a trade-off at all. Roosevelt's New Deal, and the subsequent successful decades of Keynesian policies in all the capitalist nations, had as their goal nothing more than the rescue of unregulated capitalism from its own incompetence.

Let us pause for a moment in this history of liberalism as trade-offs to notice a fundamental continuity. Both the nineteenth-century trade-off of the older liberal human rights for economic plenty, and the twentieth-century marginal reversal which appeared to sacrifice growth to rights, were justified in the interests of the atomic individual. The first was justified on the ground that it would maximize the aggregate wealth of the nation, or the Gross National Product, and thus maximize aggregate individual utilities. The second was justified as distributing the GNP more justly between the same atomic individuals. The focus of both was on material utilities. Individual human rights were reduced to, or taken to be sufficiently provided by, a level of material utilities.

This is a far cry from the original vision. It treats the individual as a maximizing consumer, not as an exerter and enjoyer of innate capacities. It has more of Milton Friedman than of John Milton. The old liberalism of liberty, equality, and fraternity was replaced by its shadow. Welfare state liberalism invokes an ambiguous liberty and a token equality but has forgotten fraternity.

This is not good enough to sustain liberal democracy in the later twentieth century. For now the desire of the individual for some human stature has acquired new dimensions. The degradation of work under managed capitalism and modern technology has led to a new demand for meaningful work, work in which the individual may feel he or she is part of something worth while, in which there is some play for an instinct of workmanship. And the degradation of the environment by air and water pollution, and of the neighbourhood by capitalist development, is engendering a new demand for meaningful community.

Rights—human rights—are coming back into academic fashion, with less of a time-lag than might have been expected—I mean less than the normal time-lag between the real world of articulate public demands on the one hand and academic consciousness on the other. The current academic recognition of rights, as against material utility, has indeed come hard on the heels of the newly articulate women's movement, the environmental movement, the burgeoning community movements, and the demands for workers' participation in management decisions. But the academic theorists can scarcely be said to have caught up yet. For most of us still start from the maximizing atomic individual. We may define the utilities to be maximized more broadly than mere material satisfactions, but then so did Bentham, who listed many non-material satisfactions as on a par with material ones but proceeded to measure them all in terms of money income. Bentham's catalogue of non-material satisfactions went only skin deep: he stuck with the individual as maximizer of utilities.

How many of us twentieth-century liberal-democratic theorists have done much better? Not many. On the whole, we still start from the nineteenth-century atomic individual, and this leaves us in the same dilemma as John Stuart Mill, unwilling to trade off capitalist individualism for developmental individual rights. Mill saw no need for such a trade-off because he did not, in mid-nineteenth century, see that the two were incompatible. We now have no excuse for failing to see this. What then is to be done? Can any of the values of original seventeenth-century liberalism be saved, which would now require coming to terms with the newer needs of liberal democracy? If not, we should have no illusions. If the liberal-democratic capitalist state cannot meet the demands now being made of it, it is likely to relapse into a less democratic or anti-democratic state, to trade off the remaining human rights, more decisively this time, for the rights of capital. Can this be prevented? I am not competent to assess the chances in practice. But it can at least be said that this depends on the strength and mobilization of the democractic forces against it. And that in turn will depend on the clarity of the understanding which the people who must make up those forces have of the underlying issue. If they take their views at second hand from newspaper columnists and political commentators in the other media there is still some hope, for those sources are a little more aware now than they were a decade ago of the underlying issue. And we may hope that they will become still more aware as depression and pollution deepen. Without relying entirely on a trickle-down effect we may think that there is still a role for political theorists, scribblers whose ideas do sometimes percolate through to the media.

What then should the theorists do? The main thing, I suggest, is to abandon the received idea that liberalism consists of, or can be accommodated by, trade-offs. I have argued that liberalism, for the last two centuries or so, has been seen by its exponents and practitioners as one or another kind of trade-off. And one might add that this is apt to get worse: the present popularity of trade-off terminology, as an easy formulation of all sorts of political and economic and personal decisions, makes it easier than ever to cast liberalism in trade-off terms. But if we look closely at the implications of the trade-offs I have imputed to liberalism we can see that they are now indefensible and stultifying.

Liberal theory and practice in the nineteenth and twentieth centuries, I have said, has comprised two main trade-offs. The liberalism of the nineteenth century—classical capitalist liberalism—traded off individual rights which had been seen as fundamental by the revolutionary seventeenth- and eighteenth-century liberals, in favour of maximum aggregate utilities. The welfare liberalism of the twentieth century, readmitting some minimum material rights but still tied to capitalism, asks us to accept a different trade-off. It asks us to forgo the democractic responsibility which was demanded by liberal-democratic theory in the nineteenth century, though not attained in practice, and which is now being redemanded by popular pressures on a wider front, that is, in both government and industry (or, if you like, in both consumption and production). It asks us to forgo this in the interests of individual freedoms which are thought to be endangered by any full measure of democracy. In my view, both these trade-offs must now be abandoned: the first as morally and practically inadmissible in twentieth-century circumstances, the second as wrongly conceived. Let us look at them in turn.

We have already noticed, in the nineteenth-century shift from individual human rights to aggregate utilities, that the utilities thus enthroned were reducible to *material* utilities. This was morally defensible at that time, when it could be argued that more, and more developed and varied, human needs could be met by the enormous expansion of productivity which capitalism both promised and performed. Even the sharpest critic of capitalism, I mean Karl Marx, argued that it would generate fuller and richer human needs.[2] But that moral justification is no longer available, since practice has shown, as indeed Marx held to be inevitable, that capitalism cannot go far to fulfill those needs for everyone. But may not utilitarian liberalism be made tenable by its acknowledging that the utilities to be maximized must be taken to include many non-material satisfactions? What if we include as individual utilities, and hence as the units of aggregate utility, such human needs as self-respect, being esteemed by one's fellows, having some con-

[2] Marx, *Grundrisse* (trans. M. Nicolaus: Penguin), pp. 325, 409–10.

trol over one's own life and choices, and the sense of belonging to some community with a shared set of values? There are surely adequate logical grounds for including these: utility, after all, has always been measured in terms of the satisfaction of felt wants; so, to the extent that such desires as these are felt wants, they must be counted as utilities.

Some liberal theorists have already moved in this direction, and it is a promising departure. But we must notice that this will not be enough if we still think in terms of a common measure between the material and non-material utilities, as the trade-off concept obliges us to do. For we are then right back at Bentham, who held that the only common measure of all pains and pleasures is money.[3] Again we may refer to Marx, who pointed out that in capitalist society use-values (utilities) can only be expressed in the form of exchange values (money).[4] Marx in effect endorsed Bentham's insight, but saw it as true only in capitalist society. And indeed it is in that society to a peculiar extent that non-material use values do have to be weighed against material ones by the same measure: most of the basic choices most individuals can make must be trade-offs of non-material for material values. No doubt, in any society where work that is no satisfaction in itself must still be done for the income it will bring, individuals will perforce measure, at the margin, such human values as esteem, autonomy, and community against material utilities. To that extent we shall still be caught up in trade-offs. But in a post-capitalist society which made full use of the productive technology now available, such trade-offs would not be so pressing. For the labour force as a whole it would no longer be a matter of daily bread: the margin would have moved. Thus in the measure that capitalism is transcended, those individual trade-offs will be less required. And in the measure that individual trade-offs are less required there will be less reason for social policy as a whole to be calculated in trade-off terms.

It would be idle to speculate on the possible extent and timing of what I have loosely called the transcendence of capitalism. But if and when it comes it will be due to cumulative popular pressures, already in evidence, which arise, not from relative deprivation in the usual sense, but from the very want of esteem, autonomy, and community. I conclude not only that liberal democracy needs to abandon trade-off thinking, but also that there is some possibility of its doing so.

We have still to consider the second main liberal trade-off, that of welfare-state liberalism, which, while admitting a minimum level of

[3] W. Stark (ed.), *Bentham's Economic Writings* I. 117.
[4] Marx, *Grundrisse*, pp. 415–16.

material rights, is still tied to capitalism. Welfare liberalism asks us to forgo any fuller measure than now exists of democratic control, or democratic responsibility of governments and corporate controllers to those whom they rule, in the interests of individual freedoms which are thought to be endangered by any fuller democracy. This way of thinking is to be found among liberals both of the centre and the right. The former, building on such insights as John Stuart Mill's, fear something approaching a tyranny of the majority which would inhibit all manner of individual freedoms for self-development. The latter are concerned primarily with freedom of economic enterprise, which they hold to be essential to individual autonomy. They must of course extend the right of free enterprise to the modern corporation, which is now the dominant enterpriser, but this can easily be played down and conflated with individual freedoms. We are asked, then, to trade off democratic control for individual and corporate freedoms.

Now there can be no doubt that democratic control is incompatible with the corporate freedoms that are needed for maximum capital accumulation. Capital has every reason, for the sake of its own liberties, to resist democratic control. An unlimited property right cannot co-exist with democracy. A democratic optimist may point out that legislatures and courts have already made serious inroads into the unlimited property right. But the greater the inroads, the more strenuously do the spokesmen of capital seek to tie freedom of property to all the other individual freedoms.

The liberal democrat who sees through this special pleading may yet well be concerned with the apparent incompatibility of democratic control and individual freedom in general. Democracies have often been intolerant. Is not any fuller or more direct democracy a clear threat to that individual autonomy, that ability to make some significant choices for oneself, not to be wholly subject to heteronomous control, which is one of the highest human values? The desire for such autonomy cannot be dismissed as simply a residue of bourgeois ideology, for that autonomy is also central to Marx's vision of the fully human being. Nor does such autonomy entail an anarchist position, for there is a difference between submission to *any* authority and submission to the rules necessary for any social life provided the rules are imposed by a consensus, or even a democratic majority, reached by full and equal effective participation of all who are to be subject to the rules.

Still, is there not a danger that such full democracy would deny some essential human right? Should we not therefore be willing to trade off any fuller democracy for individual rights? This question is not easy to answer, but we can make a start by clearing away some confusions. Let us notice first that not far beneath the surface of this distrust of democracy is the fear of big brother, the fear of a totalitarian state. There are grounds enough for that fear in the record of twentieth-century Communist and Third World regimes which began with a vision of full, often direct, democracy but have ended in a military/bureaucratic state which effectively denies individual liberties. The mechanism of that denial was the suppression of the civil liberties—freedom of speech, publication, and association, and freedom from arbitrary arrest or detention.

The first thing at stake, then, for the liberal democrat, is the preservation of civil liberties. And we may hope that by now the liberal democrat will have seen this, will have seen that democracy requires the civil liberties. Without them, democracy is a travesty. Their suppression in an immediate post-revolutionary period may be defensible, but it is not defensible in any longer run. Without the civil liberties there can be no responsiveness of governments to the will of the people, for then that will has no way of making itself felt.

Thus civil liberties and democratic responsiveness are not alternatives to be traded off: rather, democratic responsiveness requires civil liberties. The reverse proposition, that civil liberties require democratic responsiveness, may seem more doubtful. A significant measure of civil liberties can be, and in the Anglo-American tradition has been, maintained by Whiggish oligarchic regimes, even to the present. But what of the future? I think we must expect that in the measure that increasing tensions develop between popular demands and capitalism's ability to meet those demands, the last safeguard of civil liberties is likely to be democratic pressures. If this is so, the supposed incompatibility of civil liberties and democracy is false: each will require the other.

Moreover, the broader fundamental rights to respect, autonomy and community also require, and are required by, any effective democracy. They are unlikely to be achieved or defended without democractic responsibility of rulers to ruled. And they are required by any society which takes equality and fraternity to be essentials of democracy.

Another confusion remains to be cleared up. Those who fear a fuller measure of democratic control sometimes point out that there will be a need for some trade-off of democratic control against efficiency in governmental implementation of democratically determined social goals. Everything cannot be left to self-governing small communes. It must be conceded that our complex modern economies, if they are to continue to provide even their present level of satisfactions, require a substantial measure of central direction and control. We cannot take refuge in a vision of petty-bourgeois production, or a society of autonomous co-operatives. Indeed, as long as there is some scarcity relative to the enriched human needs which we envisage, there will need to be some central authority to ration the available goods by some criterion of distributive justice. But a need for such central control is not inconsistent with democratic responsiveness. On the contrary, that central control will only work if the social goals are democratically determined. There will, while any scarcity prevails, have to be some trade-off between governmental efficiency and direct democratic control, at least as long as those who are exerting democratic pressures are unaware of the difference between short and long-run benefits to themselves. Central direction of the economy must devolve on bureaucrats, but it is not beyond imagination that they may be instructed by and held responsible to democratically elected councils at all the requisite levels from local to national.

Where does this leave us? What if all the trade-off thinking we have found in liberalism right up to the present is admitted by political theorists to be no longer tenable? What if we theorists do abandon it? Everything then will depend, it seems to me, on the extent of popular consciousness of the reasons for abandoning it. Without a revolution in that consciousness, nothing much is likely to be done. We seem to be back to relying on trickle-down effects, from the theorists to the media to popular consciousness. But we should not despair. Time is on our side. The incompetence of late-twentieth-century capitalism works for us.

Let me, in concluding, revert to a point I put forward earlier. I suggested that trade-off formulations of social issues often depend on the covering up by the stronger party, and the overlooking by the weaker party, of possibilities which transcend the trade-off choice. A corollary is, that in the measure that the stronger and weaker parties change places, the former stronger party loses its power to formulate the issues in trade-off terms, and the former weaker party, by the very activity which has brought it ahead, may gain the insight to transcend the trade-off choice.

Within the theory and practice of liberalism up till now, possessive liberals have been the stronger, and developmental liberals the weaker, party. If, but only if, those positions are reversed will liberalism be able to grow out of its trade-off constrictions and make common cause with other currents of humanism.

CHAPTER 5

Do We Need a Theory of the State?[1]

1. The Question Clarified

My question is not whether we need a theoretical understanding of the political process in modern states, but whether we need a theory of the state in the grand manner of the acknowledged 'great' theories, ranging in modern times from, say, Bodin and Hobbes to Hegel and the nineteenth-century juristic theories of sovereignty, and on to the less 'great', but in intention equally grand, theories of Green and Bosanquet and such twentieth-century thinkers as Barker and Lindsay and MacIver.

There is, I assume, no question that in order to understand the operation of contemporary states we need theories of the political process in our own liberal-democratic states (and, if we are to be comprehensively informed, in Communist and Third World states as well). There is no lack of such process theory, especially of the liberal-democratic state: that is where the bulk of the work of political scientists has been done for the last few decades, and it has given us a new understanding of the role of parties, pressure groups, and bureaucracies, the determinants of voting behaviour, and so on. The general theory that has come to prevail, which may be described as a pluralist-élitist-equilibrium theory, may be thought not entirely adequate even as a descriptive and explanatory theory—it has come under considerable fire by a number of radical liberal-democratic theorists,[2] and W. J. M. Mackenzie has recently pointed out its failure to take account of political violence.[3] But my concern here is not with an appraisal of that empirical theory, except in so far as the rise of such theory may throw light on the reasons for the decline of grand theories of the state.

My concern is whether we now need something more than theories of the political process. Do we need a theory of the state in the grand

[1] First published in the *European Journal of Sociology*, XVIII (1977).
[2] e.g. several of the contributors to three collections: Charles A. McCoy and John Playford (eds.), *Apolitical Politics* (1967); William E. Connolly (ed.), *The Bias of Pluralism* (1969); Henry S. Kariel (ed.), *Frontiers of Democratic Theory* (1970).
[3] In his *Power, Violence, Decision* (1975).

tradition? The hallmark of the grand theories is that they all tied the state back to supposed essentially human purposes and capacities, to a supposed essential nature of man. In doing so they were of course both descriptive and prescriptive or justificatory. They sought both to explain what the actual state was, and to show either that it was justified or necessary or that it ought to be and could be replaced by something else. But what I would emphasize is that they did relate the state normatively to supposed essentially human purposes. Do we again need such a theory of the state? To raise this question is of course to assume that we haven't got an adequate one now. I make that assumption, and will support it as I go on.

An answer to this question depends obviously on who 'we' are. I take 'us' to be those living in late-twentieth-century liberal-democratic societies, and especially those of us whose vocation is the study of politics. Do we, as so defined, need a new theory of the state? I shall argue that some of us do and some of us don't.

We may I think divide this whole constituency into distinctively different parts. I suggest that a threefold classification is appropriate for the purposes of our question.

(1) In the first category I put those who on the whole accept and uphold the existing liberal-democratic society and state, with no more than marginal reservations or hopes that they can be made somewhat better, within the same framework, by, for instance, more informed citizen participation, or less or more welfare-state activity. This category includes the bulk of the contemporary empirical theorists and, at a different level, some normative theorists who may be called philosophic liberals.

(2) The second category is those who accept and would promote the normative values that were read into the liberal-democratic society and state by J. S. Mill and the nineteenth- and twentieth-century idealist theorists, but who reject the present liberal-democratic society and state as having failed to live up to those values, or as being incapable of realizing them. This includes the bulk of contemporary social democrats and those socialists who do not accept the whole of the Marxian theory.

(3) The third category is those who reject both the idealist normative theory and the present liberal-democratic society and state, and would replace both of them totally by Marxian theory and practice.

I would not claim that this classification is exhaustive. One might, for instance, make a separate category of those who take a philosophical anarchist position, who need at least a theory of the negative relation of the state to essential human purposes: they need a theory of the state in order to abolish the theory of the state. Nor would I claim that the lines between the three classes are entirely clear and sharp, but I think the classification makes some sense in the context of my question.

2. Negative and Positive Needs for a Theory

I shall now argue that those in the first category do *not* need a grand theory of the state, and that those in the second and third categories *do* need one.

(1) The first category, as noted, includes both most of the current empirical theorists and some normative liberal theorists. Their needs may be considered separately.

(a) The empirical theorists generally claim to have abstained from any value judgement about the processes they are analysing. But their theories usually have strong commendatory overtones. If they had really avoided all value judgement they would not only not need a grand theory of the state: they would be incapable of one, for such a theory is always normative as well as explanatory. But since a value judgement is at least implicit in their theories, one might argue that they do need a theory of the state after all: that they need to make explicit and to develop the values that underlie their theorizing (which would enlarge their empirical theory to the dimensions of a theory of the state).

But they cannot afford to do this. Having rejected the 'classical' liberal-democratic model of John Stuart Mill and Green and their twentieth-century followers, with its humanistic striving—rejected it as unrealistic (that is, as beyond the capacities of the average twentieth-century citizen)—the empirical theorists cannot afford a theory which would tie the state back to some supposed essential nature of man. For to do so would be to reveal that they have reverted to a Benthamist or even Hobbesian model of man as possessive individualist. They have, it is true, come some distance from the Hobbes–Bentham model of society as a series of freely competitive market relations. They have been able to adjust their model of society to some of the realities of managed capitalism. But even managed capitalism presupposes maximizing market man, and they have accepted, even while they have refined, that concept of man. That concept of man has, I believe, become increasingly morally unacceptable in the late twentieth century. Thus for the empirical theorists to go on to a theory of the state would be to expose the inadequacy of their basic assumptions. It would endanger their position as the spokesmen for liberal democracy, since their model of man and society is becoming morally repugnant to increasing numbers of people within the liberal democracies, as well as in the world at large. I conclude that the empirical theorists do not need, at least in the sense that they cannot afford, a theory of the state.

(*b*) What of the contemporary normative theorists, the philosophers who have concerned themselves with the political, of whom the most influential and widely discussed at present are Rawls and Nozick?[4] They also are working with a market model of man and society. There is of course a sharp difference between them: Rawls is happy with the welfare state encroachments on unalloyed capitalism and can even contemplate their extension, whereas Nozick argues for a return to the minimal state. But they both endorse the fundamental relations of capitalist market society and its property institutions. And since they assume maximizing market man as the norm, they need not go behind that to inquire into the nature or potential of man and to relate that to the state. They need not be concerned with any necessary or historical relation of the state to society or to supposed essentially human purposes or capacities. They do not need a theory of the state, but only a theory of distributive justice, i.e. of the just distribution of 'primary goods' (Rawls) or of 'holdings' (Nozick), or a theory of liberty (i.e. of the allowable or morally desirable amount and kind of individual liberty). The state can be treated as simply an agent which does or should subserve the principles of justice or liberty which the theorist argues for.

It thus appears that the philosophic liberals, like the empirical theorists, do not need a theory of the state. It may even be suggested that contemporary philosophic liberals cannot afford to attempt one. The philosophic liberals of fifty or ninety years ago (MacIver, Barker, Lindsay, Green) could afford to, because, while they accepted capitalist society in its main outlines, they were far from accepting the market model of man. Having a broader vision of the nature of man, they could and did try to relate the state to it. But not much can be done, beyond what was done by Hobbes and Bentham, to relate the state to market man. An attempt to do so in any depth would reveal the time-bound quality of the basic assumptions about man.

Rawls, indeed, in the last part of his book, does go on to a different vision of the nature of man, as a creature who wants to maximize his 'primary goods' only as a means to realize a plan of life or concept of the

---

[4] John Rawls, *A Theory of Justice* (1971); Robert Nozick, *Anarchy, State and Utopia* (1974).

good, or to develop his capacities to the fullest. But Rawls does not explain how this is consistent with the market model of man on which his whole theory of justice is based. He is thus left unable to go beyond a theory of distributive justice to a theory of the state.

(2) Turning to my second category—those who accept the humanistic values read into liberal democracy by Mill and the idealists, but who reject present liberal democracy as having failed to realize those values— it can readily be seen that they do need a theory of the state. For, believing as they do that the state should embody certain moral values which they find not now realized by liberal-democratic states, they are committed to a theory at once normative and explanatory, i.e. to a theory in the grand tradition which relates the state to human needs, capacities, and potentialities. It follows that they need a new theory of the state in the measure that the theory they have inherited from humanist liberals and idealists (ranging from Mill and Green to Barker, Lindsay, MacIver, etc.) is inadequate.

That the inherited theory is seriously inadequate is sufficiently evident from the ease with which it was eclipsed in mid-twentieth-century by the empiricists' theories. Its eclipse was due chiefly to the fact that the explanatory or descriptive side of the twentieth-century traditional theories was demonstrably inaccurate. Citizens of the Western democracies did not behave like the rational, informed, and even public-spirited citizens postulated by the traditional theory.

The traditional theorists might have defended their position by pointing out that they were not trying to describe and reduce to operative principles the political process in those contemporary states commonly called democracies, but were trying to deduce the essential requirements of democracy from their vision of human needs and capacities. This gave them the concept of democracy as a kind of society and political system which would provide the equal possibility of self-development by all. To complete that defence it would only be necessary to argue, as they did, that people are capable of a degree of rational and moral self-development which would enable them to live in a fully democratic society and to participate actively in a fully democratic state.

But such a twofold defence could not save their position. For while they were indeed seeking to show 'the essentials of democracy' rather than merely to describe existing democratic institutions, they did present the existing liberal democracies as having met the essential requirements in substantial degree. They did so, it may be surmised, because they were all more or less explicitly concerned to build a case for existing democracies *vs* existing or threatened dictatorships. So they had to argue that the existing Western democracies had the root of the matter in them. To do this they had to examine the existing system of parties, pressure groups, and public opinion formation, and argue that it did, however roughly, come up to the essential requirements. So they had to argue not merely that people were capable of the required degree of rational and moral self-development but that they had already reached it or nearly reached it.

They thus came up with a pluralist theory of society and of the democratic state. The democratic state was an arrangement by which rational, well-intentioned citizens, who indeed had a wide variety of different interests but had also a sense of a common interest or even a 'general will'[5] could and did adjust their differences in an active, rational, give-and-take of parties and interest groups and the free press. The empirical theorists were able to show that most citizens of liberal-democratic states were far from being such active rational participants, and were thus able virtually to demolish the traditional theory.

Perhaps the fundamental weakness of the traditional theorists was that they had unconsciously adopted the notion of the democratic process as a competitive market. They did not make the market analogy explicitly, as the empirical theorists were to do. That analogy implies a society made up of narrowly self-interested maximizing individuals, and this was incompatible with the traditional theorists' image of man as a moral being whose essence was to be realized only in the self-development of all his human capacities. But their model of a plural society was a market model.

This in itself could not have led to their eclipse by the empirical theories, for the latter were openly based on the market analogy. But it has meant that late twentieth-century liberal attempts to revive the traditional theory have run aground. For they have adhered to the pluralist model, while the society for which they are prescribing has become increasingly less plural. As I shall argue,[6] late capitalist society does still exhibit some measure of pluralism, but its amount has shrunk and its character has changed as the corporate-managed sector and the state-operated sector of the economy have encroached on and diminished the competitive market sector.

I conclude that contemporary theorists in my second category do need a new theory of the state.

[5] R. M. MacIver, *The Modern State* (1926), p. 342.
[6] Below, pp. 71–3.

(3) Turning finally to those in my third category, I think it is clear that they also need to develop a theory of the state. Marx's theory was certainly normative as well as analytical, and the role of the state was crucial to his whole theory, yet he did not provide more than fragments of a theory of the state. Lenin did rather more, but however appropriate his conclusions were when he wrote they are not adequate for the late twentieth century. It follows that contemporary Marxists do need a new or more developed theory of the state than they have inherited. And Marxist scholars in the West have in the last decade become very much aware of this and have plunged vigorously into the effort to provide it. There is already a substantial body of work, to mention only the almost simultaneous books by Poulantzas (*Pouvoir politique et classes sociales*, 1968) and Miliband (*The State in Capitalist Society*, 1969), the subsequent extended debate between them in the *New Left Review*, and independent discussions in Europe and America, which have taken the matter farther and in different directions, as in the Genoa conference sponsored by the Council for European Studies in 1973,[7] in the papers in the journal *Kapitalistate* (1973–) produced by a joint editorial group now mainly in the US but drawing on many West European writers; and in seminal books by Jürgen Habermas[8] and James O'Connor.[9] This work, still continuing, is in the tradition of grand theory.

A grand theory of the state, I have said, has to tie the state back to the supposed nature and purpose and capacities of man. At the same time it has to take account of the underlying nature of the society in which that state operates. The contemporary Marxist theorists do not both, though with varying emphasis on the two aspects. Indeed much of the dispute amongst them may be reduced to that difference of emphasis, some of them building on Marx the humanist and some on Marx the analyst of capitalist society. The two can be, and to a limited extent have been, drawn together by the recognition, growing since the publication of Marx's *Grundrisse*, that there is no dichotomy between Marx the humanist and Marx the analyst of capitalism. But there are still deep divisions on how or whether Marx's own position on the role of the state in capitalist society, which he never fully spelled out, can be applied to the relation between state and capital in 'late' or 'advanced' capitalism.[10]

[7] Published in Leon N. Linberg *et al.* (eds.), *Stress and Contradiction in Modern Capitalism: public policy and the theory of the state* (Lexington, Mass., 1975).

[8] *Legitimation Crisis* (Boston, 1975), first published in German in 1973.

[9] *The Fiscal Crisis of the State,* (New York, 1973).

[10] e.g. the controversy between Miliband and Poulantzas, and other controversies in the *New Left Review*, e.g. Gough (NLR 92) and Fine and Harris (NLR 98).

I cannot attempt here either to summarize this body of work or to assess it. But I think it is worth asking its relevance to those who are in my second category: what if anything can be learned from it by those who do not accept, or do not fully accept, the classical Marxian position, and yet do not accept the existing liberal-democractic society and state as morally adequate? I find the question worth asking because I place myself in category 2, and because I believe that some contemporary liberal theorists are inclined to move from category 1 to 2. So I shall in the rest of this chapter preach to them. A preacher must have a message. My message is, learn from those in category 3.

3. Contemporary Marxist Lessons for Liberal-Democratic Theory

I think there is a lot to learn from them. For they do see more clearly than most others that what has to be examined is the relation of the state to bourgeois society, and they are examining it in depth. In this they are repairing a great defect of the twentieth-century traditional liberal theory, which accepted bourgeois society but did not examine the implications of that acceptance.

One characteristic of the grand tradition, if we take it from the seventeenth to the early twentieth century, is its move from a materialist to an idealist view of man and society. One cannot say that that move is the measure or the cause of the twentieth-century eclipse of the grand tradition: Hegel's theory of the state is, after all, rather more penetrating than Locke's or Bentham's, for Hegel knew that he was talking about the state in bourgeois society. But one can say that the later idealists increasingly departed from that insight, that they played down or virtually dismissed, or at any rate could not cope with, the fact that it was the bourgeois state, or the state in bourgeois society, that had to be dealt with. They sought to rise above that specific society, not by examining any inherent momentum in it which might be transforming it or leading to its supersession, but on the contrary by reaching for an archetype of all human society.

So they were led to what I have called a bow-and-arrow theory.[11] This is rather like the economic theory which, seeking a similar level of generality, defines 'capital' so broadly as to cover both modern capital and the primitive hunter's bow and arrow. Such a concept of capital is formally intelligible: the bow and arrow and the capital of a modern corporation are both the outcome of their owner's abstinence from immedi-

---

[11] Cf. 'Bow and Arrow Power', *The Nation* (19 Jan. 1970).

ate consumption of some of what they produce or collect, or, it you like, are both the product of their investment decisions. But such a broad concept misses the difference between the two, a difference not just in degree but in kind, and so obscures some essentials of modern capital.

Here, as in theories of the state, the judgement of what are the essentials—the judgement whether the common features are more important or less important that the specific features—is a value judgement (though the theorists often fail to see that it is). For on this choice depends the extent to which the resulting theory will implicitly justify or criticize the specific modern phenomena. The bow and arrow gives you abstinence as the source of capital and so makes modern capital a wholly admirable thing. Similarly with the state. The common feature may be seen as provision for a human desire for the good life or the full life, or for community: in that case the state, any state, is a wholly admirable thing. Or the common feature may be seen as the need for an authority able to hold in check the contentious nature of man: in that case, the state, any state, is still an admirable thing.

It is true that the twentieth-century traditional theorists for the most part offered a theory of the liberal-democratic state rather than a theory of the state as such. But they are still caught up in bow-and-arrow thinking in so far as their argument moves from 'the good state' to the liberal-democratic state, justifying the latter as the best or the nearest possible approach to the former.

In any case the twentieth-century traditional theorists have not given much attention to the specific nature of the state in capitalist society. It was easy for them to abstract from the capitalist nature of their society, since the one theory which made that central—i.e. Marxist theory—was, through most of the twentieth century, unsatisfactory in several ways. It was associated with dictatorships. It was doctrinaire. And it took so little account of twentieth-century changes in the nature of capitalism that it could readily be dismissed as less realistic than a refined pluralism which talked of 'post-industrial society', countervailing powers, and so on. This refined pluralism is not entirely wrong, but it does distract attention from the fact that the motor of our system is still capital accumulation (as should be evident from a glance at any financial paper). And the presumption must surely be that this is bound to have a lot to do with the nature of the state.

The new generation of Marxist scholars in the West has largely overcome the defects just mentioned. Their work is not doctrinaire, and it is mainly concerned with the changed and changing nature of capitalism in the late twentieth century. They are, that is to say, examining the necessary and possible relation of the liberal-democratic state to contemporary capitalist society, which has changed in significant ways since Marx, and since Lenin.

It seems to me that that relation is crucially important to those of us who want to preserve some liberal-democratic values. And I do not see anyone other than the contemporary Marxist scholars examining it in any depth. That is I think reason enough for us to try to learn from them. Let me draw attention to some of their main theses, and suggest some implications for liberal democracy.

1. They assume, with Marx, (*a*) that the human essence is to be realized fully only in free, conscious, creative activity; (*b*) that human beings have a greater capacity for this than has ever hitherto been allowed to develop; and (*c*) that a capitalist society denies this essential humanity to most of its inhabitants, in that it reduces human capacities to a commodity which, even when it fetches its exchange value in a free competitive market, receives less than it adds to the value of the product, thus increasing the mass of capital, and capital's ability to dominate those whose labour it buys.

This is the philosophic underpinning of Marx's whole enterprise. It is difficult for a liberal to fault (*a*) and (*b*), the assumptions about the nature and capacities of man: virtually the same position was taken by, for instance, Mill and Green. And it is short-sighted for the liberal not to give serious consideration to the validity of (*c*)—the postulate of the necessarily dehumanizing nature of capitalism—for that does not depend on the ability of Marx's labour theory of value to explain market prices (which has been the main complaint about his economic theory) but only on his path-breaking argument that the value produced by human labour-power (i.e. by its capacity of working productively) exceeds the cost of producing that labour-power, the excess going to the increase of capital. This position is more difficult to fault than is the adequacy of his price theory.

The present Marxist theorists of the state start from Marx's ontological and ethical position, and go on to consider where the state fits in to this depiction of capitalism and, given that, what are the prospects that late capitalism (which is supported, but also encroached on, by the state) may be transcended, as Marx believed capitalism would be. In pursuing this inquiry they are naturally concerned mainly with the analysis of late capitalism, taking as given the ethical dimension of the problem. Because of that concern, their work may not appear to be in the grand tradition of theories of the state—may appear, that is to say, not to be relating the state to a concept of essentially human needs and capacities. But this is an appearance only. Their work, no less than Marx's, is designed to serve the realization of the supposed essential nature of the human species. So if, in my ensuing description of some of their leading arguments, I appear to move out of the realm of philosophy and political theory into that of political economy this must not be taken to derogate from their role in the grand tradition.

2. It is assumed that an indispensable job of the state in capitalist society is to maintain the conditions for capitalist enterprise and capital accumulation. This, however, does not imply that the state is the lackey or the junior partner of the capitalists. Indeed, for reasons that will be mentioned,[12] the state is seen to have been moving away from being a mere superstructure and to have attained a significant degree of autonomy. The point is rather that, given a state's commitment to capitalist enterprise as the mainspring of the economy, the holders of state office must in their own interest maintain and support the accumulation process because the state's revenue, and hence the power of the state's officers, depends on it. Hence in a democratic capitalist society, although the electorate determines who shall hold office as the government, governments are not free to make what use they might like of their constitutional power. The government must stay within the limits imposed by the requirements of the accumulation process, limitations generally imposed on social-democratic governments through the mediation of the permanent bureaucracy and sometimes of the military.

3. The need to promote accumulation has, with the maturation of late capitalism, required the state to take on a new range of functions, the performance of which has raised new problems. The change has been from the minimal support provided by the classical liberal state (law and order, contract definition and enforcement, and some material infrastructure—roads, canals, ports, etc.), to what might be called maximal support.

Five areas of new or greatly increased support may be identified, all apparently necessary: (*a*) the whole apparatus of the welfare state, which, in providing cushions against unemployment and against the costs of sickness, old age, and reproduction of the labour force, takes some of the burden that otherwise would have to be met by capital, or if not so met, would endanger public order; (*b*) the Keynesian monetary and fiscal management of the economy, designed to prevent wide swings

[12] Below, pp. 71-3.

and to maintain a high level of employment; (*c*) greatly increased infrastructure support, e.g. in technical and higher education, urban transportation systems, urban and regional development schemes, public housing, energy plants, and direct and indirect state engagement in technological research and development; (*d*) measures to prevent or reduce the damaging material side-effects of particular capitals' search for profits, e.g. measures against pollution and destruction of natural resources. These, like the welfare-state measures (which are designed to prevent or reduce the damaging human side-effects of particular capitals' operations) are increasingly required in the interests of capital in general, but do limit the profits of some particular capitals; (*e*) a large new apparatus of state-imposed marketing boards, price-support schemes, wage arbitration procedures, etc., designed to stabilize markets in commodities and labour and capital.

It is held that while all those new supports are required, they also in some measure undermine what they are intended to support. The extent to which, and the way in which, each does so is different.

The first does not directly undermine it, but since it has to be financed out of the profits of capital, it reduces accumulation (or at least appears to particular capitals to reduce it, though it does so only in comparison with a wage-capital relation that is now insupportable). And it may be said to reduce it by preventing capital driving such a hard wage bargain as it could otherwise do. The second appears to reduce it by limiting the very swings on which capital had relied to redress in the downswings the gains made by labour in the upswings. This reduction, like the first or even more so, is partly illusory: it leaves out of the calculation the loss of accumulation in prolonged periods of depression. The third, like the first, is very costly, and the cost must be met out of the profits of capital. This is not all loss to capital, since some of these state activities, notably technical education and research and development, do increase the productivity of private capitals. But the balance sheet is hard to draw. The fourth is a clear interference with the freedom of particular capitals. The fifth is perhaps the most serious, in that it replaces freely made market decisions by political decisions. Particular capitals (and particular segments of organized labour) are compelled to accommodate their conflicting private interests to public decisions. This erodes the ability of capital to make the most of itself, and reduces its accumulative freedom.

All five of these state activities, then, while they are necessary supports to capital in general, i.e. to the continuance and stability of a capitalist economy, are or appear to be opposed to the interests of particular capitals. And between them these activities may undermine the accumulation of capital in general: by enlarging the public sector, they take an increasing proportion of the labour force and the capital flow out of the operation of the market, and so may reduce the scope of capital accumulation. But this need not amount to a net reduction in private accumulation. It will not do so in so far as the state is thereby taking over unprofitable but necessary operations and/or is absorbing the cost of looking after that part of the labour-force which technological change has made redundant.

4. The late capitalist economy is seen as consisting of three sectors: (*a*) the corporate oligopolistic sector, the firms in which are largely able to set their own prices and thus can both invest heavily in technological advances and afford high wages, so that the labour force in this sector is relatively advantaged; (*b*) the remaining competitive private sector of smaller firms, unable to afford either, so that they can neither accumulate through technological investment nor provide secure wages; which leaves its labour force relatively disadvantaged; and (*c*) the public sector, the labour force in which—blue- and white-collar and managerial—has its compensation set by political rather than market bargaining, and which is consequently relatively advantaged: if 40 per cent of the whole labour force is employed in the public sector, so is roughly 40 per cent of the whole electorate.

5. The combined effect of the increase in the role of the state, and the fragmentation of labour and capital into the three sectors, has been a considerable alteration in the classic capitalist relations of production and the relation of capital to state. The economy has become politicized, reverting in this respect to the pre-capitalist pattern. Yet the state now relies, for its own power, on maintaining capitalist accumulation. And since the state is now democratic it faces two new difficulties: it must reconcile the requirements of accumulation with the demands of the electorate, and it must extract an increasing revenue from capital to finance its support of capital and its response to the electorate.

Consideration of these difficulties has led outstanding contemporary Marxist scholars to develop theories of crisis. Habermas writes of the need for the accumulation-supporting state to legitimate itself to the electorate: this is the 'legitimation crisis'. O'Connor finds a contradiction between the state's need for expanded revenues and the maintenance of capital accumulation: this is 'the fiscal crisis of the state'.

'Crisis' suggests either the impending breakdown of capitalism or, if capitalism is to survive, the breakdown of democracy. Either of these is evidently now possible, but I shall suggest not necessary. Certainly the late capitalist state has a legitimation problem which the earlier capitalist state did not have. Earlier, when the market, not the state, was and was seen to be responsible for the economy and all the recurrently damaging effects of depressions, and when the market allocation of rewards was thought to be either fair or inevitable, the state had no great difficulty about legitimating its existence and its performance of its minimal functions. But now that the state takes, and is seen to take, heavy responsiblity for the economy and its side-effects, the state has a serious legitimation problem. And as the state takes on more (and more expensive) support functions, it does run into a series of fiscal crises which could lead to the breakdown either of democracy or of capitalism. The outcome of the legitimation and fiscal crises is indeterminate, since it depends not on objective forces alone but also on conscious political action.

I have touched on only some of the main points in the contemporary Marxist analyses of the state. But it is already evident that there are suggestive lines that should be followed up. The prospect of any measure of liberal-democratic values surviving, and the question of the possible means of assisting such survival, are more complex than indicated so far. In the following section I want to suggest some amendments and extensions of the Marxist analyses sketched above which may carry us a little way towards a more adequate view of the liberal-democratic problem.

4. Ways Ahead?

I want now to argue (1) that as a result of the changes set out in paragraphs 3 and 4 above, the nature of the legitimation problem has already been altered; (2) that the same changes have set up a new kind of pluralism, a pluralism in reverse; (3) that the possibility of saving any liberal democracy depends on a change of consciousness, which depends on a public awareness of the real nature of the new pluralism; and (4) that this sets an agenda for a useful theory of the state in the late twentieth century.

(1) The legitimation problem has changed. For the advanced capitalist state can fairly easily legitimate itself to three very large sections of the public.

(*i*) The whole personnel of the public sector, who owe their relative job security and relatively higher wages to the state. It is true that increasing numbers of public employees, both blue- and white-collar, have recently unionized (and some have become quite militant) in order to protect their position against government retrenchment policies, from which they would otherwise be among the first to suffer. But they are still more secure and better paid than employees in the competitive private sector.

(*ii*) The recipients of welfare-state benefits. These also, especially those most in need, are taking to organizing, in welfare rights groups, tenants' organizations, and community coalitions of various sorts, to secure the benefits that are theirs on paper or to demand further benefits. This makes them seem adversaries of the state. But they are still clients, and the more they win the more dependent they are.

This is not to say that they are inert dependants of the state. No one would doubt that the rise of the elaborate welfare-state in all the Western democracies was due to the political strength of organized labour, whether expressed in trade-union pressure on established parties or in the rise to power of social-democratic and labour parties. But to say that it was their power which created the welfare state, and which requires its continuance, is not to deny that they, as well as the unorganized and redundant labour force, all of whom are its beneficiaries, are now dependent on the state for the continuance of their benefits. The relation is reciprocal: they created the welfare state, but now they are its creature.

They still indeed have the potential of turning out a government which fails to give them what they have come to count on, but since the failure will have been due to the fiscal crisis of the state this will not improve their position as long as they accept the need for private capital accumulation. So, to the extent that they are kept by the state they will keep the state.

(*iii*) The strongly organized part of the labour force in the private sector. They can see quite well that they owe their relatively advantaged position to the state's support and subsidization of their employers' operations, and they consequently can readily accept the legitimacy of the state which so serves them.

Against this it may be argued that they, along with the employees of the public sector, are the first to bear the brunt of the now apparently endemic wage and price controls, and that they have shown by their strenuous opposition to such devices no great affection for the state which imposes them. It must be granted that in the measure that such controls are permanent the state will have more difficulty in legitimating itself to them. But realistic trade unionists in the advantaged sectors can see that in spite of this their gain from the continuing state support and subsidization of their employers outweighs their loss from what they hope will be temporary wage controls.

These three categories together make up a substantial majority of the electorate. As long as the state can find the money, it will have no great difficulty legitimating itself to them.

But what about (*iv*)—the holders and operators of capital? Is not the real crisis of legitimation, now, whether the state can legitimate itself to them, rather than to the electorate? To speak of this as a problem of legitimation is to stretch the concept of legitimation considerably beyond its original and its current Marxist usage. There, it has been a matter of the state, or of a virtual merger of state and corporate capital (which merger is seen as parasitic on the body politic), having to legitimate itself to the body politic by mystifying its true nature.

I do not mean to deny the realism of this position. To have seen the problem of legitimation in this way was a substantial step forward. But I suggest that the problem I have put is also a problem of legitimation. For the state, whether or not it is seen as jointly parasitic with capital, is still sufficiently different from corporate capital to have to justify its activities to the latter. If the state cannot do so, capital can go on strike: can make impossible, or severely reduce, the state's operation of all the mechanisms which now legitimate the state to (*i*), (*ii*), and (*iii*), and can thus accentuate the legitimation problem. This seems to me to be the central problem of the advanced capitalist state. But I think it not insoluble.

The state may be able to legitimate itself to (*iv*) in either or both of two ways. (*a*) By persuading particular capitals that the state's support of the interests of capital in general is more to their long-term benefit than would be the state's leaving particular capitals to their own devices. This persuasion is not impossible: it has succeeded at least once within recent memory: after sustained opposition to Roosevelt's New Deal, particular capitals finally admitted their benefit from it. A similar persuasion, at the higher level that would now be required, might succeed again.

(*b*) By making each of the particular capitals (and the particular segments of organized labour) conscious, if they were not already sufficiently conscious, that each of them, separately (not firm by firm, but industry by industry) owes whatever prosperity it has to the state's continuing subsidization and regulation. In all those industries in which the state has become an indispensable subsidizer (which includes virtually the whole of the big corporate sector), the state has considerable leverage: it can hold them separately to ransom by threatening to reduce or withdraw its support. Hog producers, wheat producers, steel producers, automobile and tank producers, textile producers, armaments producers (and their unionized labour forces), and so across the whole of the organized private sector, all of them may be more or less *bought* by guaranteed prices, guaranteed purchases, tariff protection, government contracts, tax concessions, or other preferential treatment.

(2) This treating of particular capitals separately is, I suggest, the heart of the new pluralism of the late twentieth century. The new pluralism both is narrower than the received pluralist model, and embodies a reverse pluralism. Its difference from the presently received pluralist model is evident. It is not the give-and-take between the government and a myriad of voluntary associations and interest groups, which was supposed to give every alert citizen, ranged in one or more of those associations, a fair share of influence on government decisions. The received model was, indeed, never entirely realistic. For, while treating the democratic political process as something like a market (which it was), it abstracted too far from the capitalist nature of the society. It did not recognize that the requirements of capital accumulation set limits to, and set the direction of, the state's response to the plural pressures. And it was inclined to treat all pressures as eliciting from a neutral state responses proportional to their size. But at least the received pluralist theory was, for the era of full market competition, fairly accurate in one respect: the state acted upon pressures, but did not itself do much to interfere with those pressures.

This, I suggest, is what is now changing. The pressures which now operate effectively on the state are those of particular organized capitals (and particular segments of the organized labour force) each of which depends upon the state for the security and preferential treatment it enjoys. This is what has given the state such relative autonomy from capital in general as it now has. Pluralism, in this respect, has gone into reverse: the state now pluralizes capital, by its ability to reduce or withhold favours to separate particular capitals.

There is indeed some measure also of what might be called reverse-reverse pluralism. Multinational corporations can play off particular national states against each other for favours, because of their ability to move their capitals. And in federal nation-states, capitals can play off different levels of the state, i.e. of governments and bureaucracies. But the national state's ability to pluralize capital is still significant.

It is true that the whole range of interest groups celebrated by the received pluralist theories is still alive, and that it comprises not only corporate producers' interest groups and various levels and segments of organized labour, but also many others—professional groups, women, ethnic minorities, scientists, banks, universities, the performing arts, even publishers, not to mention all the ethical groups concerned with such issues as abortion, capital punishment, marijuana, and privacy. They all engage in lobbying. Their voices are heard, but are they heeded? It is a reasonable presumption that all of the demands of these other interest groups which would cost money will get increasingly short shrift as the fiscal difficulties of the state increase. The interest groups that will remain at all effective will be those organizations of particular capitals (and the parallel labour groups) who can show that the state's continuing support of them is essential to the maintenance of the capitalist economy. And these are the ones that the state can separately hold to ransom. The undoubted fact of increasing concentration of capitals in particular industries does not affect this: the greater the concentration in any one industry—steel, textiles, wheat, oil, cement, communications—the stronger their lobbies become, but the more they are dependent on the state's favours, and the more they can be held in line.

The new pluralism, then, is a two-way affair: the new element is the ability of the state to pluralize capital. The pressure groups that will continue to be effective are those corporate and labour groups over which the state has a stranglehold, if it wishes (or is financially compelled) to use it. And it is likely to have to do so increasingly.

There is a historical parallel to this state pluralization of capital. Just as the capitalist state from the beginning expropriated the communal life of earlier society, atomized it, absorbed the powers people had exercised together, and used those powers to rule the people in the interests of capital in general;[13] so now, in advanced capitalism, the state has to add a parallel operation—it absorbs from particular capitals some of their powers (i.e. some of their revenues, and hence of their ability to accumulate) and uses that power, still in the interests of capital in general, to make particular capitals dependent on the state.

[13] Cf. Alan Wolfe, 'New Directions in the Marxist Theory of Politics', *Politics and Society* (1974), pp. 145 ff.

It is probable that this reverse pluralism, and the relative autonomy of the state, will increase as the state gets more deeply involved in the management of the economy, the stabilization of markets, and the subsidization of production and prices. And the relative autonomy of the state from capital will also be aided as the public sector expands and moves more of the whole labour force and capital force from market determination to political determination.

There are, however, clear limits to any such increase in relative autonomy, *as long as the electorate continues to support, i..e. not to reject, capitalism.* So long as capitalism is thus maintained, the state is still dependent on the accumulation of private capital: even with the enlarged public sector, the state must still operate within the limits of maintaining capital accumulation in general, however skilful it may be in manoeuvering between particular capitals. The state in a capitalist society cannot be a neutral uncle: it must serve the interests of capital.

(3) What becomes of the relative autonomy, how it will be used, depends now, I suggest, on whether, or how rapidly, the public becomes conscious of the real nature of advanced capitalism and is moved to political action to alter it. The relative autonomy of the state, or the reverse pluralism, will not be the spark of any such new consciousness: the spark can only be an awareness of the incompetence of advanced capitalism and of the state which supports and tries to manage it: the relative autonomy of the state is merely the conduit in which the spark may ignite.

There are already some indications of such a new awareness. There is a growing disbelief in technology as the cure-all, in view of the damaging uses to which managed capitalism puts it (pollution and ecological destruction). There is a growing restiveness within the labour force over its subordination to organization and technology (wildcat strikes and shop-steward militancy). And as the state runs into deepening fiscal difficulties, there is likely to be increasing restiveness among some of those sections of the public who were said earlier (above, pp. 68-9) to be fairly easily persuaded of the legitimacy of the state as long as the money held out, i.e. (*i*) workers in the public sector, as expenditures on hospitals, schools, etc., are cut back, so reducing or cancelling their relative job security, and (*ii*) some of the recipients of welfare-state benefits, e.g. the unemployed, as budgeting provision for them is reduced.

Such disenchantments with the capitalist state are important, for the maintenance of capitalism requires not only all the legal and material supports which the state now supplies, but also a general acceptance of the rightness of the system, or at least a belief that there is no acceptable alternative. In the earlier days of capitalism, *competition* was presented as 'the natural system of liberty', beneficial to all. In advanced capitalism, *organization* takes the place of competition as the universal benefactor: the 'post-industrial', technological, managed society is presented as the solution to all problems and contradictions[14] In the measure that this belief in organization crumbles, there opens up a possibility that political action can put human purposes above capital purposes.

This is indeed no more than a possibility. The belief, reinforced as it is by the ubiquitous presence of the corporate sector in our channels of political socialization, may not crumble. And the inherent tendency of the Western party system to obfuscate basic issues[15] works to prevent a public consciousness of the real nature of the political economy of capitalism. But there is at least the possibility that reality will break through.

(4) It is here that a realistic and normative theory of the state can contribute, by delineating both (*i*) the necessary and necessarily changing relation of the state to capitalist society, and (*ii*) the limits of the possible relation of the capitalist society and state to essential human needs and capacities. The contemporary Marxist theorists are doing a good job on (*i*), but in most cases to the relative neglect of (*ii*).

To reinstate the tradition of grand theories of the state, further work on (*ii*) is now needed. The theory of the state does have to come back from political economy to political philosophy, though it can only come back effectively in the measure that it has probed political economy. It also needs more empirical and theoretical work on human needs, wants and capacities,[16] and a full re-assessment of the behaviouralists' findings about the present processes of political socialization from childhood through adulthood.[17]

A euphoric vision is that all this can be done co-operatively, or in friendly rivalry, by the adherents of my categories 2 and 3. This is not impossible, for some of the contemporary Marxist scholars whom I have placed in category 3 have been led by their analyses to doubt the

---

[14] Cf. Ernest Mandel, *Late Capitalism* (1975): 'Belief in the omnipotence of technology is the specific form of bourgeois ideology in late capitalism' (p. 501).

[15] Cf. my *The Life and Times of Liberal Democracy* (Oxford, 1977), ch. III, 3.

[16] Cf. the essays by various authors in Ross Fitzgerald (ed.), *Human Needs and Politics* (New York, Pergamon, 1977).

[17] A striking beginning has been made in Alan Wolfe's article cited above. Cf. his *The Limits of Legitimacy* (Free Press, New York; Collier Macmillan, London, 1977).

present relevance of the classical Marxian revolutionary prescription, adherence to which was the main thing that separated category 3 from 2. A still more euphoric, even utopian, vision is the coinciding of a merger of 2 and 3 with a significant shift of theorists from 1 to 2. If that were to happen, the political-theory profession could be said to have entered the late twentieth century.

CHAPTER 6

Human Rights as Property Rights[1]

In these days, when we are all becoming more concerned about the way we are using up our natural resources, polluting our environment, and destroying the ecological balance of nature, it still seems to some that there is an insuperable difficulty in doing anything effective about it. The difficulty is that any effective action about it seems to contradict one of the central concepts, and to undermine one of the basic institutions, on which all the advanced Western or liberal democratic societies are based: the concept and institution of individual property.

This contradiction, of course, will have to be resolved, or compromised or patched up or papered over, by our politicians. That is what we elect politicians to do.

But can the political theorist make any contribution to the resolution, beyond the papering over of this contradiction? He can perhaps say something useful by drawing attention to some demonstrable facts: to the fact that the concept of property has changed in several ways, not only as between ancient and medieval and modern societies but also within the span of modern market society; and to the fact that it is now again perceptibly changing and may be expected to change still further. He may also inquire whether changes are now needed, in order to make the concept of property consistent with a democratic society, and if so, whether such changes are impossibly difficult. I shall suggest that they are needed, and that they are not impossibly difficult.

I shall only try to deal with a few of the changes that have in fact occurred; only with those whose implications for the present and future seem to be most worth looking at. I shall look at four changes.

(1) The first change I want to notice may appear to be only a lexicographical or dictionary change in the usage of the word 'property', but I think it goes deeper. As late as the seventeenth century, it was quite usual for writers to use the word in what seems to us an extraordinarily

---

[1] First published in *Dissent*, Winter 1977.

wide sense. John Locke repeatedly and explicitly defined men's properties as their lives, liberties, and estates. For Hobbes, the things in which a man had property included 'his own life and limbs; and in the next degree, (in most men), those that concern conjugal affection; and after them riches and means of living.'[2] One's own person, one's capacities, one's rights and liberties were regarded as individual property. They were even more important than individual property in material things and revenues, partly because they were seen as the source and justification of individual material property.

That broad meaning of property was lost in the measure that modern societies became fully market societies. Property soon came to have only the narrower meaning it generally has today: property in material things or revenues. The reason is fairly obvious: with the predominance of the market, every individual's effective rights and liberties, their effective ability to develop their own persons and exercise their capacities, came to depend so much on what material property they had that the very idea of property was easily reduced to the idea of material property.

(2) A second change in the concept of property, which came at about the same time, was even more striking. It was, like the other, a drastic narrowing of the concept: this was a narrowing even of the concept of material property.

From the earliest ideas of property, say from Aristotle down to the seventeenth century, property was seen to include both of two kinds of individual rights: both an individual right to exclude others from some use or enjoyment of some thing, and an individual right not to be excluded from the use or enjoyment of things the society had declared to be for common use—common lands, parks, roads, waters. Both were rights of individuals. Both rights were created and maintained by society or the state. Both therefore were individual property.

From the seventeenth century to our own time, the idea of property has generally been much narrower. It has largely been narrowed to the first right—the right to exclude others.

True, we do have such things as national parks. But it is not usual to think of these as property at all. It is more usual to think of them as something set aside from the property arena. The only time we treat any part of them as property is when the state does turn some part of them into property in the narrow sense, by giving some person or corporation the right to exclude others from some use of them, as when it sells or

---

[2] *Leviathan*, Ch. 30, pp. 382-3 (Pelican Classics, Macpherson, C. B. ed.).

leases logging or mining rights. Certainly we don't ordinarily think of every citizen's right of using a national park as part of each citizen's individual property. So it seems accurate to say that the moden concept of property is pretty well confined to the right of an individual or corporation—a natural or artificial person—to exclude others from some use or enjoyment of some thing.

(3) A third, related change is a further narrowing—from property as an exclusive right merely to use and enjoy some thing, to property as an exclusive right both to use and to dispose of the thing: a right to sell it to somebody else, or to alienate it. This is now taken so much as a matter of course that it may seem surprising to say that it came as a change a few centuries ago. I shall postpone a description of this change till I come to look at the causes of this and all the other changes.

(4) A fourth change in the concept of property is also a narrowing, and also dates from about the same time. It is not as important as the others, but it is worth noticing. It is a change from property as a right to a revenue to property as a right to things (including the things that produce revenue). A further description of this change I shall also postpone until I look at causes.

To sum up these changes, we are left with a modern concept of property as an exclusive individual right to use and dispose of material things.

Obviously, some further change now is needed to make our narrow concept of property consistent with a democratic society. Property as an exclusive right of a natural or artificial person to use and dispose of material things (including land and resources) leads necessarily, in any kind of market society (from the freest, most perfectly competitive one, to a highly monopolistic one), to an inequality of wealth and power that denies a lot of people the possibility of a reasonably human life.

The narrow institution of property is bound to result in such inequality, in any society short of a genetically engineered one that would have ironed out all differences in skill and energy. Even if you started from complete equality of property, the operation of exclusive and disposable property rights would soon lead to some getting more than others; and the more one gets, the easier it is to get still more, so that, at least after free land runs out, a relatively few people get the exclusive right to the bulk of the land and working capital. Those who are left without any, or without enough to work on or work with on their own, then have to pay the others for access to it. There is then a continuous net transfer of part of the powers of the nonowners to the owners.

This is an inevitable consequence of turning everything into exclusive property and throwing everything into the market. This is clearly inconsistent with one of the first principles of a democratic society, which I take to be the maintenance of equal opportunity to use and develop and enjoy whatever capacities each person has. Those who have to pay for access to the means of using their capacities and exerting their energies, and pay by making over to others both the control of their capacities and some of the product of their energies—those people are denied equality in the use and development and enjoyment of their own capacities. And in a modern market society, that amounts to most people: almost everybody except the fortunate few who are, as professional people, more or less independent and more or less exempt from that transfer of powers.

This kind of inequality is not only inconsistent with the democratic principle: it also contradicts one of the basic justifications of the very institution of individual property, namely, that human needs cannot be met without that institution. It can easily be demonstrated that, granted an equal right to life, everyone needs such an amount of individual property, in the means of life and in access to the means of labour, as will ensure the continuance of his or her life. And on any acceptable notion of human rights, this requires more than a right to bare physical subsistence. It requires an equal right to such means of life and means of labour as any society, at its given level of command of Nature, can provide.

The very nature of human beings, then, requires individual property of two kinds. One kind, some property in the means of life, is a property in consumable things. This must be an *exclusive* property: I must have the right to exclude you from my shirt, from my dinner, from my toothbrush, and from my bed.

The other, a property in the means of labour—that is, in the resources, the land and capital, access to which I need in order to exert my energies and utilize my capacities—this does not need to be an exclusive property. It can, equally well, be the other kind of individual property—the right *not to be excluded from* some use or enjoyment of something.

The validity of the case for property as a necessary human right depends, then, on whether we take property in the modern narrow sense, or in the more extended and more natural sense of an individual right both to some exclusive property and to some non-exclusive right of access to the remaining natural resources and the accumulated capital of a given society. If we continue to take it in the modern narrow sense, the property right contradicts democratic human rights. If we take it in the broader sense, it does not contradict a democratic concept of human rights: indeed, it then may bring us back to something like the old concept of individual property in one's life, liberty, and capacities.

So it becomes important to consider what are the chances of our moving away from the narrow concept of property to the broader one that seems required by any concept of human rights. And to do this we must look at the causes of the narrowing, and see if, or to what extent, they still operate.

Each of the four narrowings that I singled out can be shown to be a pretty direct result of the rise of the competitive capitalist market economy, which, as it became predominant, brought within its sway things, and people, and the values that are embodied in concepts.

I have mentioned the obvious source of the first narrowing (the narrowing from an individual property in one's life, one's person, capacities, rights and liberties, as well as in the material means of life, to merely property in the material means of life). This, I said, was an evident result of the fact that, with the predominance of the market, all individuals' effective rights, liberties, ability to develop their own persons and exercise their own capacities came to depend so much on the amount of their material property that it was not unrealistic to equate their individual property with their material property.

What about the second narrowing, from an individual property in both the individual right *to exclude others* from the use or enjoyment of some thing and an individual right *not to be excluded from* the use or enjoyment of some thing, to merely the right to exclude others?

This also was required by the full market economy. To the extent that the whole job of deciding what was to be produced, and how the whole product was to be divided between people, was to be done by the market, rather than by custom or prescription or political authority—to that extent, all rights in material things, including land and other natural resources, not to mention rights in one's capacity to work, had to be made marketable and brought into the market. And clearly only the exclusive rights can be marketed. The right not to be excluded from some use or enjoyment of some thing cannot, by its very nature, be marketed. So, of the two earlier kinds of individual property—the right to exclude others, and the right not to be excluded by others—the second virtually dropped out of sight with the predominance of this market, and the very idea of property was narrowed to cover only the right to exclude others.

Much the same explanation applies to the third narrowing of the concept of property, which was a further narrowing even of the notion of property as an exclusive right in material things. Before the full market society came to prevail, a great deal of property in land and other material things was a right to exclude others from some use or enjoyment of the thing, but not a right to dispose of it. The right to use, or enjoy the revenue from, a parcel of land or a corporate charter or a monopoly granted by the state did not always carry with it the right to sell that property. But a full market economy requires that everything be marketable. If the market is to do the whole job of allocating resources and labour between possible uses, then all resources and labour have to become marketable. Individual rights in them all must include the right to buy and sell, the right to dispose of or alienate. As the capitalist market economy grew, it was expected to do, and did do, most of the whole job of allocation. So it was not surprising that the very concept of property was narrowed to property as exclusive alienable rights.

The fourth narrowing, less important than the others but worth noticing, dates from the same period and can be seen to have come about for similar reasons. It is the change from property as rights in things and in revenues to property as rights in things, or, if you like to sharpen the contrast, a change from rights in revenues to rights in things. This change in the concept reflected a change in the facts. Until the emergence of the capitalist market economy, most individual property had in fact been a right to a revenue rather than a right to a thing. The great bulk of property had been property in land, and, at least in the case of substantial estates, that property was seen as a right to a revenue rather than a right to the land itself, the more so because, as we have noticed, the land itself was often not in the owner's power to sell. Another large segment of individual property was the right to a revenue from such things as corporate charters, monopolies, and various political and ecclesiastic offices. Whether these properties were saleable or not, they were obviously rights to a revenue rather than rights to any specific material things.

Then, with the rise of the capitalist market economy, the bulk of actual property shifted from often nontransferable rights to a revenue from land, charters, monopolies, and offices, to transferable rights in freehold land, saleable leases, physical plant, and money. Property became predominantly a right to things.

Now let us recall that the point of looking at the causes of the various narrowings of the concept of property was to enable us to consider the chances of the concept of property being broadened again. What are the chances of any such broadening? In considering this, it will be convenient to treat the four narrowings in reverse order.

(*Re* 4) Property is already being reconceived as a right to a revenue. As capitalism has matured and has become subject to much regulation, and as the distribution of its whole annual product has become subject to some redistribution by welfare-state measures, the most realistic description of most people's property is coming to be a right to a revenue: either (a) the right to earn an income or (b) the right to an income not currently earned. Category (b) comprises all investment income, including pension rights (which are increasingly widespread in blue-collar as well as white-collar sectors); and all the many kinds of income provided by the state, in money or in services, such as family allowances, unemployment benefits, health services, and old-age benefits. Category (a) comprises (i), for self-employed people, from doctors to independent taxi operators, the right to earn an income from the practice of their skills. This often comes down to the need for a licence: the licence itself is a property, sometimes (like taxi licences) a saleable property. And (ii), for wage earners, it comes down to a right to a job. This right is increasingly being asserted by organized labour. It is an assertion of a right of access to the means of labour, no matter by whom owned. That right is increasingly seen as a property. The perception of it as a property is quite a big change in the concept of property.

(*Re* 3 and 2, which we may take together) The concept of property as an *exclusive, alienable* right (in things and revenues) is already beginning to change. The right to a job that is now being asserted is clearly not an alienable right; and it is also not, at least in principle, a right to exclude others, so much as it is a right not be excluded from something, namely, from access to society's accumulated means of labour (although it may be, in the immediate short-run, a right of organized labour to exclude unorganized labour from that access).

Another form of individual property, which by now is well over the horizon, is also neither an exclusive nor an alienable right: this is the 'guaranteed annual income', or the income provided by a 'negative income tax'. One or other of these schemes is almost certainly going to become increasingly implemented, both for technical economic reasons and because of democratic political pressures.

Besides these two factors that are now perceptible in our society, there is a reason to expect more change away from the idea of property as merely exclusive alienable rights. The reason is that this concept was necessary only to the extent that the market was expected to do the whole work of allocation of resources and labour and products and rewards. But in our age of regulated and managed capitalism (regulated by the state and managed by corporations engaged in less than perfect competition), the market is no longer expected to do this work. The state now does, and in future will increasingly do, much of the work of allocation. As it does so, there will be less and less need of the concept of property as nothing but exclusive alienable rights. So there is now some prospect of our breaking out of the second and third narrowings.

(*Re* 1) What are the chances of reversing the first narrowing: of recapturing, on a higher level, the idea that individual property is much more a matter of property in life and liberty, in the use and development and enjoyment of human capacities, than it is merely a matter of rights in things or revenues? What makes this now possible is the inevitability of increasing productivity, with less need for current compulsory labour, through technological advance. Technological advance is inherent in capitalism: it is virtually the only means of survival of the oligopolistic firm within the capitalist economy, and the only means of the survival of that economy as a whole in its competition with the Communist economies. It is bound to make current labour less and less necessary to provide an acceptable standard of life, always provided that we opt for less work rather than more things.

As current labour becomes less needed, individual property in the means of labour becomes less important, and individual property in the means of a full and free life becomes more important. The important thing becomes individual property in the means of a life of using and developing and exerting our capacities and energies.

I think it is probable, or at least possible, that there will be more demand for this kind of property. There is no certainty about this. We may just go on behaving as insatiable consumers. Our demand for the means of a full life may just be a demand for more consumer goods. But it need not be so. We may pick up again what is a very old idea, the idea that used to prevail before the market economy converted us all into consumers: the idea that life is for *doing* rather than just *getting*. You

may ask, can the right to such a full and free life of action and enjoyment be made an individual property, i.e. a legally enforceable claim
that society will enforce in favour of each individual? There is no
intrinsic difficulty about this. It may seem surprising, but the historical
record bears me out.

All societies that preceded the market society did establish and maintain legal rights not only to life but to a certain quality of life. I am
thinking of the rights of different orders or ranks—guild masters,
journeymen, apprentices, servants, and labourers; serfs, freemen, and
noblemen; members of the first and second and third estates. All of
these were rights, enforced by law or custom, to a certain standard of
life, not just of material means of life, but also of liberties, privileges,
honour, and status. And these rights could be seen as *properties*.

Of course these were very unequal rights: they adhered to rank or
class. They had to be unequal, since there was never enough to go
around. But the point is that there was no difficulty in having the right
to a certain quality of life made into a legally enforceable claim of the
individual, i.e. an individual property.

And now, in the twentieth century, one factor has changed: there is
enough to go around, or will be if we make intelligent use of our
knowledge of Nature, i.e. of our presently possible productive technology. So it now becomes possible to assert an equal right, for everyone, to a certain quality of life, certain liberties to develop and enjoy the
use of our capacities. And it becomes possible to treat these rights, just
as the earlier unequal rights were treated—as property, i.e. enforceable
claims of the individual.

If you have followed me so far, you may still wonder what is the point
of treating the right to a quality of life as a property right? Why not just
put it forward as a human right? The reason seems to me quite com-
pelling. If it is asserted as a human right separate from the property
right, the whole prestige of property will work against it rather than for
it. We have made property so central to our society that any thing and
any rights that are not property are very apt to take second place. So
I think that, given our present scale of values, it is only if the human
right to a full life is seen as a property right that it will stand much
chance of general realization.

Moralists and reformers, and writers of declarations of human rights,
have often played up human rights as opposed to property rights. I am
suggesting that this is a mistake, and that we will get further if we treat
human rights as property rights.

Obviously, this does not solve all problems, perhaps not any problems. But it does remove a mental barrier that is no longer justified or required, and so opens the way to a shift in public opinion, the sort of shift that is needed if we are to make much headway with human rights.

CHAPTER 7

Property as Means or End[1]

There are several possible ways of taking an overview of the theory of property in the Western political tradition. One is to give a straightforward historical account of the successive theories justifying or criticizing the various types and amounts of property that have been of concern to the political theorists of different eras, showing the changing grounds on which their cases were based.[2] Another is to make a logical classification of the grounds on which property has been or may be justified, and to subject each to tests of logical consistency and adequacy.[3] Another way is to start from observable changes in the very concept of property, that is, in the content put into the definition of property itself, in successive eras in the Western tradition, and to relate those changes to changing requirements of dominant and rising classes, as I have done in my discussion of the several narrowings of the concept, from an ancient and medieval concept which included common as well as private property, through an early modern one which thought only of private individual property but defined it so widely as to include the rights to life and liberty as well as to material estate, then a narrowing which confined property to a right to some use or benefit of some material thing or revenue, then a further narrowing which confined it to the right to alienate or dispose of as well as to use or enjoy material goods.[4]

These three ways of taking an overview of property do not exhaust the possibilities. I want now to try out another way: to look for any pattern that may be found in the Western tradition between treating property as a means to ethical ends or to ontological concepts of man, on the one hand, and on the other hand to treating property as an end in itself.

[1] First published in *Theories of Property: Aristotle to the Present*, ed. A. Parel and T. Flanagan (1979).

[2] As in Richard Schlatter's *Private Property, the History of an Idea* (Allen & Unwin, London, 1951).

[3] As in Lawrence C. Becker's *Property Rights, Philosophic Foundations* (Routledge & Kegan Paul, Boston, 1977).

[4] As in 'A Political Theory of Property', in my *Democratic Theory, Essays in Retrieval* (Clarendon Press, Oxford, 1973), and Ch. 6 above.

A search for any such pattern may seem a waste of time. For surely, it may be said, property has never, by any theorist, been treated as an end in itself, but always as a means to some other end— the good life of the citizen (Aristotle), the fulfilment of the will without which individuals are not fully human (Hegel, Green)—or as a prerequisite of individual freedom seen as the human essence (Rousseau, Jefferson, Friedman).

Similarly, the outstanding critics of private property (More, Winstanley, the Utopian socialists, Marx), and of unlimited private property (Rousseau), have denounced it as destructive of the human essence, a negative means in relation to an ontological end.

In all these cases property is treated as means, not as end. But it must be noticed that in the liberal utilitarian tradition, from Locke to Bentham, the *accumulation* of private property is treated as an end. For them, maximization of utilities is *the* end, and by Bentham the command of utilities is measured by material wealth. Thus maximization of material wealth (property) is indistinguishable from the ethical end: property is virtually an end in itself. And as early as Locke, the insistence that unlimited accumulation is a natural right of the individual comes close to making accumulation an end in itself.

We may then at least hypothesize a continuum from property as means to property as end, and see where this leads us. It will become evident that the means/end distinction is not symmetrical with the limited/unlimited right distinction. Aristotle and Aquinas, treating property as a means, concluded for a limited property right. Hegel and Green, also treating property as a means, concluded for an unlimited right. An explanation of this difference is required, and should be revealing. In the Utilitarian tradition there is more symmetry. From Locke to Bentham, accumulation of property, being treated as virtually an end, always meant a right of unlimited accumulation.

Before seeking a pattern in the treatment of property as means or end, it may be well to set out the limiting definition of property I shall be using. I confine myself here to private property, defined as a right, i.e. an enforceable claim, of an individual—a natural or artificial individual —to some use or benefit of some thing (land, capital, labour-power, or other commodities) or to some revenue from the position he holds in the political society, and the right to exclude others from that use or benefit. This is narrower than the perfectly intelligible and at one time prevalent definition of property embracing both private and common property—both the right to exclude others and the right not to be excluded by others. But it is broader than the narrowest definition mentioned above, which confines property to the right to dispose of as well as to use material things or revenues.

Now let us look at, or perhaps to avoid begging the question I should say look for, shifts back and forth between treating property as a means and as an end.

There will be little dispute that in the prevalent concepts of property throughout the ancient and medieval eras of the Western tradition the institution of private property was justified as a means to some ethical or ontological end. Whether the institution was seen as natural (Aristotle), or God-given (Augustine), or both (Aquinas), it was justified as a necessary means to the good life of the citizen (Aristotle), or as necessary to counteract the avaricious nature of fallen man (Augustine), or to provide for peaceable and orderly relations between individuals (Aquinas).

A change to seeing property as an end in itself is foreshadowed by Hobbes and fully implicit in Bentham. Let us look first at Bentham, then show how it is foreshadowed by Hobbes: this should enable us to trace the reasons for the change.

For Bentham the ultimate end to which all social arrangements should be directed was the maximization of the aggregate utility (pleasure minus pain) of the members of a society. And while he listed many kinds of pleasures, including non-material ones, he held that wealth—the possession of material goods—was so essential to the attainment of all other pleasures that it could be taken as the measure of pleasure or utility as such. 'Each portion of wealth has a corresponding portion of happiness.'[5] Further: 'Money is the instrument of measuring the quantity of pain and pleasure. Those who are not satisfied with the accuracy of this instrument must find out some other that shall be more accurate, or bid adieu to politics and morals.'[6] So, even without his further postulate that the highest pleasure was not in having but in acquiring wealth, he was satisfied that each individual should and would seek to maximize his own wealth without limit. The most general end, maximization of each individual's utilities, thus became indistinguishable from the general end of each individual's accumulation of material property. Property—not the institution of property, but the accumulation of property—has become an end in itself.

Moreover, Bentham recognized that wealth was indistinguishable from power, that is, power over others. 'Between wealth and power, the

[5] *Principles of the Civil Code*, Part I, Ch. 6.
[6] *Jeremy Bentham's Economic Writings*, ed. W. Stark (Allen & Unwin, London, 1952), I, 117.

connexion is most close and intimate: so intimate, indeed, that the disentanglement of them, even in the imagination, is a matter of no small difficulty. They are each of them respectively an instrument of production of the other.'[7] And 'human beings are the most powerful instruments of production, and therefore everyone becomes anxious to employ the services of his fellows in multiplying his own comforts. Hence the intense and universal thirst for power; the equally prevalent hatred of subjection.'[8]

So for Bentham, accumulation of property and accumulation of power over others are indistinguishable, and both are ends in themselves. It will now be apparent why I spoke of Hobbes as having foreshadowed Bentham's position. For it was Hobbes who from a somewhat different basis concluded that the search for power over others was the dominant end of man. I have argued elsewhere[9] that it is only where capitalist relations of production prevail—or if you like, only in a fully possessive market society—that this is the necessary behaviour of all men. We are then, I think, entitled to conclude that the shift from seeing the institution of property as a means to seeing the accumulation of property as an end comes with the rise of capitalist relations of production. And it is not difficult to see that the shift was initiated, even required, by that rise. For the essence of the capitalist market society is that the decisions about what shall be produced and how the whole product shall be allocated among those who contributed to its production are left mainly to the market forces which respond only to the calculations of the enterprisers how to increase their accumulations of capital. To justify that system of productive and distributive relations one must hold that unlimited accumulation is just. And in the Utilitarian tradition that required showing that maximization of accumulation is indistinguishable from maximization of utilities. Thus the shift to treating accumulation of property as an end was required to legitimate capitalist relations.

For Hegel and the English Idealists, accumulation of property was perhaps less clearly an end than a means. Yet both Hegel and Green treated the right of unlimited accumulation as entailed in their ultimate moral end, the realization of the human will or the consciousness of oneself as a moral purposive being. As Hegel put it, 'The rationale of

[7] *Constitutional Code,* Book I, Ch. 9, in *Works* (ed. Bowring) IX. 48.
[8] Stark (ed.), III. 430.
[9] *The Political Theory of Possessive Individualism* (Clarendon Press, Oxford, 1962), Ch. II, § 3.

property is to be found not in the satisfaction of needs but in the super-session of the pure objectivity of personality. In his property a person exists for the first time as reason.'[10] This is surely tantamount to treating property as an end rather than as a means. And the Idealists, like the Utilitarians, were driven to this because they accepted capitalist society as *the* model of civil society.

A further change in the treatment of property is evident in twentieth-century liberal-democratic theory, beginning indeed as early as John Stuart Mill in mid-nineteenth century. The move is back towards treating property as a means, not an end. It was inaugurated by the liberals' realization that their market society (which they generally failed to identify with capitalist society) had produced a working-class which would not much longer put up with the exploitation to which it was subjected, or be persuaded by the Benthamist rationale of an unlimited property right. Mill still held to a virtually unlimited right, but his twentieth-century followers increasingly recognized that that was incompatible with the end they espoused, i.e. the equal opportunity of individual self-development. So they moved towards property as a right limited in various ways by the end: property tended to become again a means rather than an end.

What of the future? Can we expect that property as a means will entirely replace property as an end? Here we must emphasize one distinction already made and introduce an additional one.

(1) Property as an institution, a set of enforceable claims (enforceable by the state or by a self-acting community), can be and has been justified as a means to some end—orderly peaceful relations between individuals, the good life of the citizen, the autonomy of the individual, the development of personality, and so on. But the institution itself, whether it confers limited or unlimited rights in things or revenues, has never been thought to be justifiable *as an end*. What can be and has been justified as an end is not the institution of property but the *accumulation* of property, specifically the accumulation of capital. Accumulation is the heart of capitalism, so much so that, as I have argued, it became indistinguishable from maximization of utilities as an end.

(2) We have been looking so far at justificatory theories, theories offered as rationales of this or that kind of property institution, with a view to shaping or confirming a desired or existing structure of property by persuading those members of the society whose opinion counted

10   *Philosophy of Right*, §§ 235-6; cf. T. H. Green, *Lectures on the Principles of Political Obligation*, § 213.

that the structure in question was just or legitimate. The theories were openly avowed: no concealment was necessary as long as those whose opinion counted were, or saw themselves as, beneficiaries of the structure. So from Aristotle to say Bentham, the successive prevalent theories were those which supported the structure of property that was required by successive modes of production—slave, feudal, nascent and expanding capitalist.

If this correspondence between theory and practice still held, one would expect that now, with capitalism globally contracting and under heavy pressure in its homelands, the theory of property accumulation as an end in itself, indistinguishable from the end of maximization of utility, would disappear. And indeed as an avowed theory it has virtually disappeared. Yet as long as our Western societies continue to rely on capitalist incentives as the motor of production, they will have to sanction accumulation of capital as an end. The predictable result is increasing obfuscation. For property theory must then sanction accumulation as an end while concealing that it is doing so.

I do not suppose deliberate falsification by the writers who do and will touch on property theory. They may, especially if they start from a position of ethical liberalism, be unaware of the constraint imposed by the accumulation factor, or may conceal if from themselves. A few will justify modern property simply on grounds of prescriptive right. But most will justify some institution of property as a means to some further end—justice, efficiency, freedom, consumers' sovereignty, or whatever —and will deduce the desirable types and limits of property from that end. Such an exercise can be carried out honestly and conscientiously without any clear awareness of the accumulation constraint: indeed, only with such unawareness could it be done conscientiously. But the constraint is still there: although property is treated as a means, accumulation as an end cannot be denied if capitalist property institutions, in however modified a form, are to be supported. I suggest that the recent Western tradition, from Mill or even Hegel through to Rawls and Milton Friedman, sustains this analysis, and offers us a murky theoretical prospect.

CHAPTER 8

Pluralism, Individualism, and Participation[1]

This chapter is an enquiry into the possibility of a participatory pluralist democracy emerging in Western liberal-democratic states. It is well known that the political system in those states is far from being participatory, and that the prevailing empirical pluralist theory finds this quite acceptable. Those who do not find it acceptable must consider the possibility of an alternative theory and practice.

We may start from the close relation between pluralism and liberalism. Pluralism is often identified with, or seen as the product of, liberalism—as something contained within the liberal-democratic tradition of theory, and in practice as a mechanism found in all liberal-democratic states and in no others. There is some truth in this. Pluralism, as practice and as theory, is clearly most at home in liberal-democratic states and is antithetical to one-party states. And the justificatory theory of pluralism can readily be shown to have its roots in some form of liberal individualism: indeed, I shall suggest that pluralism *is* individualism writ large.

But we ought not to be content to leave the analysis here. To do so would be to miss important dimensions of pluralism. For individualism is not a monolithic concept. It spans quite a range of assumptions about the essential nature of man. At one extreme, it takes the individual to be essentially a maximizing consumer of utilities, as in the utilitarian tradition from Hobbes to Bentham. At the other pole, it takes the individual to be essentially an exerter and developer of his/her human capacities or powers; as in the humanistic and neo-idealist theories from John Stuart Mill and T. H. Green through to the present.

Those assumptions, at the two extremes, give two quite opposite individualisms, with some grey areas in between. Corresponding to the opposite individualisms we may expect to find two opposite pluralisms, with a similarly uncertain area in between. The question is whether any

[1] A paper prepared for Section RC 17 of the International Political Science Association XI World Congress, Moscow, August 1979; first published in *Economic and Industrial Democracy* (SAGE, London and Beverly Hills), 1 (1980), 21–30.

of them may open the way to a participatory democracy quite unlike the present liberal-democratic systems.

We may proceed by calling to mind the main varieties of pluralist theory that have been significant in the last century or so, including those that are significant today. The following is obviously not exhaustive, but is perhaps sufficient for our purposes.

1. Religious pluralism. This may be traced as far back as the Reformation or seventeenth-century puritanism, and has surfaced again in our century, e.g. in the theoretical work of Figgis. The assumption of this pluralism is that the full development (primarily but not exclusively the spiritual development) of the individual requires that there be some countervailing powers against an otherwise all-powerful and stultifying state. Existing religious associations claiming independence from the state were, and still are, one of the most evident bodies to take on this countervailing task. This pluralism is narrower than those listed below: it asserts a co-ordinate moral claim of church (or sect) and state, rather than envisioning a wholly pluralistic society; but it is one of the sources of the broader humanistic pluralism listed next.

2. The nineteenth- and twentieth-century humanistic and neo-idealist pluralism of e.g. J. S. Mill, T. H. Green, Ernest Barker, A. D. Lindsay, and Robert MacIver. This is also based on the prime importance of individual development. These normative pluralists, whether in the revised utilitarian tradition of Mill or the neo-idealist tradition of Green, were not content with the quality of life and the very limited possibility of individual self-development afforded by a purely competitive market society. They held that widespread political participation was required as one means to individual self-development. They emphasized also the plural nature of every individual's interests and concerns. Each individual had many diverse interests: he was a farmer or a plumber or a doctor, a Catholic or a Jew, a lover of music or of football, a member of an ethnic minority or majority, a believer in the rights of animals or of children or of women (or indeed of men), and so on. An essential of democracy was that all these interests be represented somewhere in the political process. Without that, the richness and diversity of individual self-development would be impeded. These interests could be and were represented in the multiplicity of associations whose pressures could not be ignored by governments and political parties. The great merit of the liberal-democratic political system was that it did operate by means of these plural associations.

3. The producers' pluralism of European anarcho-syndicalism and of English guild-socialism (G. D. H. Cole and the early Laski). Here the emphasis switches to man as producer, but the normative goal is the same. Society should be governed entirely or largely by autonomous associations of people in their capacities as producers of the diverse goods and services by which modern societies live.

4. A similar pluralism is found in some current communitarian anarchist spokesmen[2] whose goal is the supersession of the state by autonomous self-governing communes.

5. The pragmatic pluralism of John Dewey, whose work was influential, especially in America, in the 1920s and 1930s. Here the central problem was seen as the need to harness science and technology to the same vision of human development, and this was thought to require a pluralistic attack.

6. Two recent liberal political philosophers may also be listed as pluralists: Isaiah Berlin, who in the revised edition of his *Two Concepts of Liberty*[3] argued that 'pluralism, with the measure of "negative" liberty that it entails' is (rather than, as in the original version, merely 'negative liberty') 'a truer and more humane ideal' than positive liberty; and John Rawls, whose vision of a well-ordered society is as 'a social union of social unions'.[4] Both theorists hold that a plural society is most conducive to the full and free development of the individual, and is needed either because of the plural nature of an individual's moral ends (Berlin) or the necessarily complementary nature of different individuals' fulfilment, in any degree, of their potentialities (Rawls).

7. Mainstream current American pluralism. While this has roots in the eighteenth and nineteenth centuries (Madison and Tocqueville), it flowered only in the twentieth century, in the work of such theorists as Bentley, Truman, Schumpeter, Dahl, Almond, and Verba, and such studies of voting behaviour as that of Berelson, Lazarsfeld, and McPhee. This pluralism disclaims any normative judgements (though they are there, not far below the surface). It is held that the current system of competing parties and pressure groups does perform, as well as is possible, the democratic function of equilibrating the diverse and shifting demands for political goods with the available

2 e.g. those in C. George Benello and Dimitrios Roussopoulos (eds.), *The Case for Participatory Democracy: Some Prospects for a Radical Society* (New York, 1971).

3 Isaiah Berlin, *Four Essays on Liberty* (Oxford, 1969), pp. 171 and lviii, n.1.

4 John Rawls, *A Theory of Justice* (Cambridge, Mass., 1971), pp. 527-9, and § 79 generally.

supply, and producing the set of political decisions most agreeable to, or least disagreeable to, the whole lot of diverse individual demands. This empirical pluralism is based on an economic market model: the party leaders are the entrepreneurs, the voters are the consumers. The voters' function is not to decide on policies but merely to choose one set of politicians who are authorized to decide the policies. This function does not require, nor does it permit, widespread continuous citizen participation. The system is lauded for its efficiency in maintaining equilibrium and providing some degree of consumer sovereignty. Its function is not to promote individual self-development but to meet the demands that individuals, as maximizing consumers, actually have and are able to express.

8. The conservative libertarian pluralism of Milton Friedman and Hayek. This also is unabashedly normative, though it gives primacy not to the vision of man as developer (as in 1 to 6) but to man as consumer. It is to be counted as pluralist because its own logic makes it so. If the mainspring of society is taken to be individual maximizing enterprise, the individuals must be allowed to combine not only in corporations but also in interest groups, in order to promote their own interests *vis-à-vis* the state.

From any such catalogue of contemporary kinds of pluralist theory, two things are evident. First, they are all extensions of some form of liberal individualism. They start from a concept of the individual as a morally self-sufficient being who seeks, and is justified in seeking, his or her own satisfactions whether as consumer of utilities or as exerter and developer of potentialities. They recognize, of course, that individuals must live in society, must exist in various relations of interdependence. But they do not commonly see the individual as the product of the relations, nor as being fully human only as a member of a community. Marx's idea of the human essence as 'in its reality . . . the ensemble of the social relations'[5] is foreign to pluralist thought, with the possible exception of Dewey, who held that 'democracy is a name for a life of full and free communion. It had its seer in Walt Whitman.'[6]

The second thing that is evident from the catalogue is that the varieties of contemporary pluralism range between opposite extremes. Two of them (7 and 8) are plainly extensions of what I have called possessive individualism.[7] They work with a model of man as a maximizing con-

5 *Theses on Feuerbach*, No. 6.
6 *The Public and Its Problems* (1927; Denver, 1954), p. 184.
7 *The Political Theory of Possessive Individualism* (Oxford, 1962).

sumer of utilities. They take human wants to be the subjective wants of individuals as they presently are, or rather, they take human wants to be the wants that are actually registered in the market (including the political market, to which the mainstream theorists have reduced the democratic political process). They see those wants as plural rather than predominantly class-divided. They take for granted that the evident plural divisions (ethnic, regional, religious, occupational, and even leisure-time preferences) in every Western society, are more important than any class division.

The possessive pluralism of (7) and (8) is simply a logical extension of the possessive individualism on which they are based. Logically, that pluralism disintegrates into the possessive individualist model of man on which the liberal tradition from Hobbes to Bentham is based. The possessive pluralists use that model, without acknowledging (or perhaps without even being aware) that they are doing so. They have neglected Rousseau's insight that every interest group is simply a combination of particular wills, opposed to, and destructive of, a general will.

The other varieties of pluralism (1 to 6) are, in greater or lesser degree, extensions of what I shall call developmental individualism. They see the human essence not as consumption of utilities but as the active exertion and development of individual potentialities. I have said that the latter theorists are 'in greater or less degree' developmental individualists. The difference of degree is related to the extent to which they accept, as a necessary limiting condition on individual development, the framework of the capitalist market economy. To the extent that they have accepted this they are caught up in an inconsistency (usually without being aware of it), for to that extent they are admitting into their analysis a market model of man as maximizer. Most of the theorists in my categories 2, 5, and 6, have done this to some extent; they have either been unaware of or unconcerned about, or unwilling to enquire very far into, the incompatibility between capitalism on the one hand and developmental individualism and pluralism on the other. This shortcoming has serious consequences for any future prospect of developmental pluralism.

One further thing should be noticed about the developmental pluralists. With few exceptions, notably some within my category 1, it has been central to their vision of pluralism, as a mechanism of individual self-development, that all the associations or groups which comprise their pluralist universe should be internally democratic and fully participatory. They have seen participation as an indispensable means to individual self-development.

We are now in a position to enquire into the prospects of pluralist theory, and of an effectively democratic pluralist system of government, in Western liberal democracies. What are the chances of developmental pluralism? They are not very good. A participatory democratic pluralism is unlikely to emerge from any internal dynamic of existing pluralisms, either of theory or of practice.

As to theory, the mainstream theorists (no. 7) either are contented with the elitist-equilibrium-pluralist model they have devised, or at least are convinced that it is the best model that Western man is capable of. And in spite of some sharp criticisms of their model by several radical liberal democrats,[8] theirs is still the dominant theory. Their only rivals in defence of market society are the conservative libertarians (no. 8). Neither of the possessive pluralisms (7 and 8) is capable of transforming itself into a developmental pluralism (which stipulates widespread participation) for they are both essentially opposed to wide participation. Of the developmental pluralisms, the most vigorous ones (nos. 1, 2, and 6) also lack a sufficient dynamic to transform themselves into an advocacy of participatory democracy, for by and large they accept a capitalist market structure, a structure which is incompatible with participatory democracy inasmuch as it leaves the allocation of material goods, and hence indirectly of political goods, largely to the determination of the market rather than to democratic decisions.

As to the practice, the Western political system, which *is* somewhat pluralist, inasmuch as it does operate partly in response to plural pressure groups, has no reason to move to a participatory democratic pluralism. The present system does indeed accommodate what I shall call 'developmental' groups and associations as well as 'possessive' ones, though it gives them very unequal weight. Let us consider in turn the possibility that either of the two kinds might contribute to a participatory pluralist democracy.

The developmental groups appear the most likely to make such a contribution, since they are by their nature actively participatory. But the present system gives them little weight. Nor can they expect to gain much weight in the present political process, for two reasons. First,

[8] e.g. Peter Bachrach, *The Theory of Democratic Elitism* (Boston and Toronto, 1967); W. E. Connolly: *The Bias of Pluralism* (New York, 1969); Carole Pateman, *Participation and Democratic Theory* (Cambridge, 1970).

unlike the possessive pressure groups, they do not usually have many friends in high places: they do not steadily infiltrate high government offices as the possessive groups do. Second, they cannot wield the most effective sanction which pressure groups have in the present system, namely, the threat of withholding services which are vital to the economy. A strike of strategic organized capital, or labour, can bring down a government: a strike of a developmental group cannot. Associations of the unemployed, of students, of women, of ethnic minorities; movements for the protection of the evironment against pollution and ecological damage; all those who want some structural changes in existing society which would open the way to more fully human development for this and future generations—none of these can employ the sanction that is most effective in dealings between pressure groups and the state, that is, the threat of withholding services which are vital to the economy. Women's services are certainly vital, in reproducing the labour force, and sustaining (as wives) the male labour force, but women perform these functions now, so that no change in their present subordinate position is needed for the functioning of the economy. And women are as unlikely now as in the time of Lysistrata to be able to organize sufficiently to withhold their vital services effectively. The other developmental groups simply have no vital services to withdraw.

So all of the developmental groups lack both an assured access to or place in the seats of power, and the ultimate sanction of withholding services vital to the economy. What those groups can do, and what many of them are doing in liberal-democratic states in our time, is to utilize the indirect sanction which is available to any of them who can organize effectively enough to change the thinking of a large number of voters, that is, can persuade a large number of voters to alter their priorities from maximization of short-run satisfactions to something that is either more public-spirited or more conducive to their own longer-run interest in the quality of life. To the extent that a developmental group can do this, whether by mass demonstrations, marches, civil disobedience, and other physical action, or more quietly by persistent propaganda, they can be effective. Politicians and governments who depend on reelection must make some concessions to their demands, whether the demands are for pollution controls, day-care centres, protection against racial or sexual discrimination, legalization of marijuana or of abortion, or whatever. All such uses of the electoral sanction can win concessions. They have done so, and probably will continue to do so. But only in the very long run, if at all, can their activities be expected to weaken the present structure of political and economic power sufficiently to bring about a really participatory system.[9]

Turning from the developmental to the possessive pressure groups we find a different and even less promising situation. The possessive groups (e.g. organized business and sections thereof, farmers—or should we now say agro-business?—doctors, and established trade unions) are sometimes in a position to use the strong sanction of threatening withholding of vital services. They can therefore be quite effective in maintaining or improving their position within the present economic structure. But that is the limit of their intentions. And they cannot themselves evolve into developmental groups for the simple reason that they cannot be internally participatory. They cannot be so because their managers, who must be in unending negotiation with the state's bureaucrats and executives and legislators, must have more room for manoeuvre than they could have if they were bound by decisions made by the rank-and-file members of the association through a genuinely participatory decision-making process.[10] For a similar reason, the political parties cannot be internally participatory as long as their main function, and that of the governments which they construct, is to reconcile monopoly capitalism with popular demands.[11]

The prospects of a participatory pluralist system thus appear rather slight. We may still ask, however, whether a fairly recent change in the power relations within capitalist society, a change not much noticed by the mainstream pluralist theorists, but strongly emphasized by such current Western neo-Marxists as Habermas,[12] Offe,[13] O'Connor,[14] and Wolfe,[15] has opened up any new possibilities. They point out that the state in capitalist society has become thoroughly involved in the economy, in a continuing attempt to save capitalism from its own contradictions or from the consequences of the short-sighted policies and activities of particular aggregations of capital. Particular capitals now depend largely on state supports and subventions, direct and indirect. This

[9] For an optimistic account of the long-run possibilities, see the discussion of the vicious circle and possible loopholes in my *The Life and Times of Liberal Democracy* (Oxford, 1977), pp. 98–108.

[10] See Claus Offe, 'Political Authority and Class Structures', *International Journal of Sociology*, II.1 (1972), 88.

[11] See *The Life and Times of Liberal Democracy*, op.cit., pp. 68–9.

[12] Jürgen Habermas, *Legitimation Crisis* (Boston, 1975; Frankfurt, 1973).

[13] Claus Offe, op.cit.; and 'Structural Problems of the Capitalist State' in *Kapitalistate* 1 and 2 (1973); 'The Theory of the Capitalist State', in L. Lindberg et al., *Stress and Contradiction in Modern Capitalism* (Lexington, 1975).

[14] James O'Connor, *The Fiscal Crisis of the State* (New York, 1973).

[15] Alan Wolfe, *The Limits of Legitimacy* (New York, 1977).

gives the state a power over particular capitals which is quite new. By threatening to withdraw its support from one or another section of capital, the state can take on an independent role. It need no longer simply respond to the pressures of particular aggregations of capital as represented in capitalist producers' pressure groups. There is now what I have called a reverse pluralism; the state is able to pluralize capital.[16] The model of capitalist society used by the mainstream American pluralist theorists is no longer as accurate as it once was.

But does this improve the prospect of developmental pluralism? I think it does not. For the state, although it is now able to attain some independence of particular capitals, is still devoted to maintaining capitalism. And in spite of the concessions the state must make in order to legitimate itself to the electorate, such a state cannot become a participatory one as long as the bulk of the electorate accepts system-stability as the overriding value. For to accept that as the highest value is to license the state—a very unparticipatory state—to continue its role as supporter of the capitalist economy, and this will require increasing state manipulation and either no change in the present level of citizen participation or a delusive change by way of a plebiscitarian state.

We are left with the conclusion that the possibility of a genuinely participatory democracy emerging in Western liberal-democratic states varies inversely with their electorates' acceptance of system-stability as the overriding value, or (which amounts to the same thing) their acceptance of the possessive individualist model of man.

[16] See my 'Do We Need a Theory of the State?', Ch. 5, above.

CHAPTER 9

The Economic Penetration of Political Theory: Some Hypotheses[1]

I propose to look at the record, over the centuries, of the varying relation between political theory, on the one hand, and on the other, ideas or assumptions that we may properly call economic. Can we explain why economic ideas at some times seem to enter into political theories only slightly if at all, and at other times are there in such strength that they may be said to penetrate the political theory? This is the economic penetration referred to in my title. If there is also in the title an implication that the penetrating quality of a political theory, its ability to get to the root of the political problems it is concerned with, depends somewhat on its economic grasp, I shall not disavow that position. But the economic penetration I am directly concerned with is the penetration of political theory by economic ideas.

I do not say 'by economic theory'. That would narrow the enquiry too far. For the relation between formal economic theory and political theory is only a small part of the relation I want to look at. It is true that some of the outstanding political theorists have also written treatises or tracts or papers in economic theory—Bodin and Locke, for instance, in monetary theory; Hume and Burke on various problems of economic policy; Bentham on public finance especially; and of course both James and John Stuart Mill produced complete *Elements* or *Principles* of political economy. But it is not always clear whether, or how much, their political thinking was shaped by their formal economic theorizing. With Bentham at least, it seems to be the other way around. In any case, I am after something broader than the relation between formal economic theory and political theory. The economic penetration I want to look at is the entry into political theories, on the ground floor or perhaps one should say in the basement, of ideas or assumptions which may properly be called economic.

I take 'economic ideas' to be ideas or assumptions about the necessary or possible relations between people in their capacity as producers of

[1] First published in the *Journal of the History of Ideas*, XXXIX. 1 (Jan.-Mar. 1978).

the material means of life. This is not, of course, recognizable as a description of the content of modern economics. In so describing 'economic ideas', I am deliberately going back to the classical political economy tradition. There is good reason for doing that, rather than seeking a starting point in modern economics. For, since the late nineteenth century, economics has largely turned its attention away from that concern which had made earlier economic thought so congruous with political thought, namely, its concern with the relations of dependence and control in which people are placed by virtue of a given system of production. Modern economics has turned instead to treating people as undifferentiated demanders of utilities. Autonomous consumer demand has been taken as the motor of the whole economic system. People are economically related to each other as demanders and exchangers of things which have market values. The central concern has become the market values of the things. Economic relations between people have in effect been reduced to relations between things: the underlying economic relations of dependence and control between people have dropped out of sight.

Twentieth-century economics has thus rendered itself incapable of illuminating political theory. Economic ideas which are confined to relations between things, or to relations between disembodied persons who appear only as the holders of demand schedules, cannot enter into political theory at any fundamental level, since political theory is about relations of dependence and control between people.

We may notice here, incidentally, one unfortunate side-effect of this change in the focus of economic theory. In giving economics a new precision, it made economics an object of admiration and imitation on the part of mid-twentieth century political scientists (who saw that they were far behind in precision). This induced political scientists to carry over into their thinking, by a superficial analogy, the impersonal market model of the marginal-utility equilibrium economists. Hence we have had in recent decades many attempts to explain the democratic political process as a political analogue of the competitive market economy. These explanations do not go very deep.[2] They read back into the political process an economic relation which had already had the real relations of dependence and control taken out of it: they read back a consumers' sovereignty model of the economy without recognizing that

[2] Cf. 'Market Concepts in Political Theory', in my *Democratic Theory: Essays in Retrieval* (Oxford, 1973), and Ch. IV of my *Life and Times of Liberal Democracy* (Oxford and New York, 1977).

the purchasing powers of various consumers are determined by their place in the relations of production.

The twentieth-century political scientists' application of economists' equilibrium models to the modern democratic process might seem to be an outstanding example of the penetration of political theory by economic ideas. But in my view, penetration is just what it is not. The equilibrium market model cannot penetrate political theory because it has abstracted from the power relations with which political theory is concerned. In what follows, therefore, I shall not treat this borrowing of an economic model by political scientists as a case of economic penetration of political theory.

To return, then, to the question what are to be counted as economic ideas for the purposes of this enquiry. Most broadly, for the reasons just given, I take them to be ideas about the necessary or possible relations between people as producers. And those relations may include, and at least from Aristotle on usually have been taken to include, relations between *classes*, distinguished by their function in the productive system or, more sloppily, by their share of the whole social product.

Moreover, since these relations between individuals and between classes require, and become congealed in, some institutions of *property*, we may take economic ideas to include ideas about the relation of property to other political rights and obligations. I say *other* political rights and obligations, because property is a right which has to be maintained politically. Property, as Bentham said, 'is entirely the work of law.'[3]

Finally, since observed relations between people as producers are apt to be read back, at a conceptual level, into assumptions about the necessary social relations between people as such, and even into assumptions about the very nature of man, we may include, under the head of economic penetration of political theory, any influence of this sort which we can see in the political theorists' models of society and of man.

How, then, are we to measure the extent of the economic penetration of political theory? As a first approximation we might say that the criterion is the extent to which actual or supposedly necessary or possible economic relations are seen as setting the *problem* of the best possible political order, or setting the problem of justice. As a closer approximation we might take the extent to which economic relations are thought to set not merely the problems, but the inescapable *requirements*, of the political system. Or, if you like, the extent to which it is thought that (to

[3] *Principles of the Civil Code*, ed. C. K. Ogden (New York, 1931), Part 1, Ch. 8, para. 1.

adapt Marx's much quoted statement), the anatomy of political society is to be sought in political economy.[4] And we may treat, as signals of such penetration, the amount of attention, or the centrality of the attention, given to property, or to class.

Another dimension that might be considered is the extent to which the economic assumptions are conscious and explicit, or more accurately, the extent to which there is a conscious and explicit assumption that economic relations set the political problem and set the inescapable requirements of a system of political obligation. But the consciousness and explicitness of this assumption cannot be used as a single measure of the economic penetration of political theories. For the economic assumptions may get into the political theory only indirectly (but none the less powerfully) at the level of a generalized model of man or of society which then determines the political theory. Since these models are generally presented as models of man or society as such, their authors cannot be expected to be conscious that they reflect any particular set of economic relations.

In looking for explanations of the varying penetration of political theory by economic assumptions, we may look first for mere correlations between the changing penetration and some other factors, and then enquire if the correlations suggest causal relations.

Looking at the whole sweep of Western political theory—ancient, medieval, and modern—one correlation suggests itself, and I shall make this my first hypothesis. I shall state it first in an oversimple form, which is irresistibly suggested by a famous formulation (about something else, namely, the division of labour) by the father of political economy. I shall accordingly offer as my first hypothesis: (1) *That the economic penetration of political theory varies with the extent of the market.* More accurately this should be, varies with the extent to which market relations have permeated the society, or, the extent to which the relations between people as producers are market relations.

This hypothesis is suggested by looking simply at the broad contrasts between ancient, medieval, and modern theory. The political theorists in all three eras paid some attention to property and class, and to economic relations more generally, but the extent of their interest in them was rather different, and they let them enter their political theories in different ways.

---

[4] *Contribution to the Critique of Political Economy* (Chicago, 1904; Moscow, 1970), Preface.

Plato and Aristotle lived in a somewhat market-oriented society, a society more market-oriented than the medieval, though nothing like as much so as the modern. Their society was still near enough to a household or simple peasant and artisan exchange economy, that standards appropriate to those could be thought natural. And the rest of the productive labour was mainly slave labour, not labour exchanged in a market betweeen labourers and buyers of labour. So the market had not permeated society, although Aristotle's strictures on unnatural money-making show that he was dealing with a fairly commercialized society. Yet Plato and Aristotle neither created man in the image of market man nor allowed that economic relations between men set the main problems or the inescapable requirements of the polity. They saw the state as not at all *for* the economy, but as having a much higher purpose. The household and the village were for the material requirements of life, the *polis* was for the good life. They did not, that is to say, allow economic assumptions to penetrate their political thinking very far. They not only put other values higher than material ones—almost all political theorists have done that—but they tried to design a polity which would provide the good life by counteracting or limiting the play of economic motives which they thought deplorable, sometimes unnatural, and at any rate always less than fully human.

Medieval society was on the whole less market-oriented; and medieval theory, at least before the rediscovery of Aristotle, showed even less economic penetration. Until then, there was not much more economic content than the Augustinian explanation of private property as punishment for, and partial remedy for the effects of, original sin.

As we move into the modern period, in which society becomes more and more permeated with market relations, with labour itself soon becoming a market commodity, the penetration of economic assumptions into political theory becomes increasingly evident. From relatively small beginnings in Machiavelli, who saw at least a necessary correspondence between a political system and the class structure, and made the class structure depend not just on amounts of property, but on the kind of property (feudal vs. mercantile), there is an increasingly full assumption that economic relations set the dominant requirements of the political system. Hobbes deduced his whole system of political obligation from a model of bourgeois man, and a model of society as a market in men's powers. Locke, seeing a man's labour as an alienable and generally alienated commodity, and consequently seeing society as naturally class-divided, was able from those assumptions to justify a class state from his initial postulate of equal natural rights. For Hume, the origin of justice, and the whole need for the state, lay in man's numberless material wants and the consequent need not only for joint labour but also for exchange and contracts. Burke and Bentham made capital accumulation through market operations the *sine qua non* of civilization, and made security for capital accumulation an essential, if not the essential, function of the state.

So one could go on. The overall pattern is fairly clear: the penetration of political theory by economic assumptions has varied roughly with the extent to which market relations have permeated society. As far as it goes, then, the pattern supports my first hypothesis.

But granting that there is historically such a correlation, is there any reason for it? Is there any causal relation? One such relation suggests itself at once. Market society requires a kind of individual freedom not found in non-market societies. It requires that men be owners of something, free to sell what they own, exempt from most of the constrictions that prevail in non-market societies. Market society encourages, even enforces, rational maximizing behaviour by all individuals. In doing so, it makes man restless. So the emergence and development of market relations raises new problems for political stability, and for any other political goals; and it is only a matter of time until perceptive political theorists see the source of the new problems, and see that they require an economic perspective.

This suggests a second subsidiary hypothesis, which must however be treated with some caution and probably should be discarded. *Hypothesis 2* is: *That the economic penetration of political theory varies with the extent of recent or current change in actual economic relations.* The actual change could of course only be correlated with the theorists' awareness of the change, which is obviously the operative factor, if we assume a standard acuteness or standard time-lag in the theorists' perception. This is a risky assumption, but it might be allowed over a very long run.

The main support for the second hypothesis lies in the contrast between the medieval period and either the ancient or the modern. There was not, comparatively speaking, much economic change in medieval society; and the comparative lack of change does correspond to the comparative lack of economic penetration of political theory in the medieval era.

But when one looks within either the ancient or the modern period, the hypothesis seems rather shaky. For in many cases it is not clear whether the theorist saw the actual economic relations which he did admit into his political thinking, as something new, something recently changed, or currently changing.

Aristotle certainly saw and deplored an accumulative mercantile society. But did he see it as a recent change? One might conclude, by inference from the position he took about unnatural money-making and about limited property, that he did not, or at least that he did not see it as an irreversible change. For what he did was to apply standards appropriate to a household or simple exchange economy to what was, by his own account of it, an advanced exchange economy driven by desire to accumulate without limit.

And in the modern period, the towering figure of Hobbes presents similar doubts. Hobbes saw (and regretted) that market man and market society were here to stay, but he fell short of recognizing clearly that this was a recent change. Now he saw it, now he didn't. His analysis of the causes of the Civil War, in *Behemoth*, does recognize it. But in *Leviathan*, and his other two theoretical treatises, there is no such recognition: in them he presents his models of man and society, which we can see are bourgeois models, as models of man and society as such. Not until the eighteenth century, in Millar and Ferguson, Hume and Adam Smith, with their three or four stages, do we find a clear recognition that society *has* changed by virtue of changes in the productive relations; and not until Rousseau do we find both a recognition that man and society have so changed, and a belief that man may change, or be changed, again.

In view of these outstanding doubtful cases, I think we should discard the second hypothesis. We are back then with nothing but the extent of the market. But this does not take us far with the changes observable within the period of the modern market society, particularly the changes within the liberal tradition from, say, Locke to the present.

There I see one fairly clear pattern of economic penetration of political theory, but it is not at all clear, at first sight, to what other factors this corresponds. The pattern is one of increasing economic penetration of liberal political theory from Locke through to Bentham and James Mill, and decreasing economic penetration from John Stuart Mill to the present. In the first period it is increasingly fully and explicitly assumed that economic relations are what set the problem and the requirements of political obligation and rights, set the problem of justice and the purpose of the state. To see this one need only compare Locke's fudge with the clarity of Hume and Bentham about the centrality of economic relations. Parallel with this, there is the increasing explanatory depth of political economy, from Petty and Boisguillebert, through the Physiocrats and Adam Smith, to Ricardo.

One is tempted to the simple hypothesis that, with the increase of the scale of the full market economy, political economy got an increasingly better grasp of the essentials of the economy, and that, correspondingly, political theorists were more influenced by political economy. Certainly the personal links became closer—Hume and Adam Smith, Adam Smith and Burke, *Économistes* and *Encyclopédistes*, James Mill and Ricardo.

Now the improvement in political economy was due to its increasing recognition of a class of industrial and agricultural (rather than mercantile) capitalists, whose share of the whole annual produce of the nation, i.e. profit, was seen to be not wages of superintendance, nor akin to rent or interest, nor merely from taking advantage of momentary terms of trade. Instead, it was seen to be the excess of the value added by the current labour which that capital employed over the wage paid. This amounts to a recognition that profit was due to the extractive or exploitive power of capital. One is therefore tempted to the further hypothesis that the economic penetration of liberal theory varies directly with the recognition, by the political and economic theorists, of the necessarily exploitive or extractive nature of market relations in a fully capitalist society.

Let us see if this is a feasible working hypothesis. An immediate objection that may be made to it is that the political economists, although they increasingly saw profit as a deduction from the value added by labour, did not see this as exploitive. It is true they did not. That is, in their formal economic theories of wages and profits there is no notion of exploitation. The reason for this is plain. *Given* the pattern of ownership which they assumed, everyone got a fair reward for what he put in. They assumed the necessary and permanent division of all modern and progressive societies into three classes: those whose income derived from (a) ownership of land, (b) ownership of capital, and (c) ownership only of their own capacity to labour. They assumed this without asking how these classes were formed. But they were well enough aware that that pattern of ownership itself was broadly exploitive. They saw that in any society in which there was a class without any material productive property (and this included the capitalist market society), that class was *used* by the others. Adam Smith made this point, and drew a political conclusion, in a well-known passage:

Whenever there is great property, there is great inequality. For one very rich man, there must be at least five hundred poor, and the affluence of the rich supposes the indigence of the many. The affluence of the rich excites the indignation of the poor, who are often both driven by want, and prompted by envy, to invade his possessions. It is only under the shelter of the civil magistrate that the owner of that valuable property, which is acquired by the labour of many years, or perhaps of many successive generations, can sleep a single night in security. . . . The acquisition of valuable and extensive property, therefore, necessarily requires the establishment of civil government. Where there is no property, or at least none that exceeds the value of two or three days' labour, civil government is not so necessary.[5]

And again: 'Civil government, so far as it is instituted for the security of property is in reality instituted for the defence of the rich against the poor, or of those who have some property against those who have none at all.'[6]

The classical liberal political theorists, whether or not they also wrote economics, were similarly outspoken, and increasingly so from Locke to Bentham. And this went along with an increasing tendency to see the job of the state as set by economic relations: in other words it went along with an increasing economic penetration of political theory. So I shall put as *Hypothesis 3: That the economic penetration of political theory varies with the theorists' recognition of the necessarily exploitive or extractive nature of market relations in a society divided into owners and nonowners of productive material property.* A glance at some highlights of liberal theory from Locke to Bentham offers some support for this.

Locke, in making the protection of property the chief end for which men enter civil society and set up government, blurred the relation by including in 'property' life, liberty, and estate. But he was explicit that it was *unequal* material property that was to be protected, and he took for granted a society in which some had nothing but their labour to sell. He combined this with a rudimentary labour theory of value, but he did not draw the conclusion that the labouring class was exploited.

Hume, more clearly than Locke, saw government as needed only when great and unequal property had been accumulated, and went beyond Locke in relating this to the emergence of the market: government is needed when the market comes to include men totally unkown to us. Hume goes on from a utilitarian justification of individual property in land and goods to an explicit recognition that *market* relations

---

[5] *Wealth of Nations*, Bk. V, Ch. 1, part ii (Modern Library edn., p. 670).
[6] Ibid., p. 674.

are the fundamental relations of society. The right of private property, the right to exchange property, and the obligation of contracts are asserted to be the three fundamental natural laws because they are all necessary for a market society. He assumed that there would always be a class of labouring poor, but he was still some way from seeing this as exploitive. That is, he did not single this out as *the* exploitive relation, though he thought almost all social relations were determined by the avidity of conflicting individual material desires.

Diderot likewise made property the *raison d'être* of the state, but went further in seeing the exploitive nature of property. Not only did he see that wage-labour is employed only because it produces a profit for the employer: he also saw that it condemned many to an inhuman existence.

Les mines du Hartz recèlent dans leurs immenses profondeurs des milliers d'hommes qui connaissent à peine la lumière du soleil et qui atteignent rarement l'âge de trente ans. C'est là qu'on voit des femmes qui ont eu douze maris.

Si vous fermez ces vastes tombeaux, vous ruinez l'État et vous condamnez tous les sujets de la Saxe ou à mourir de faim ou à s'expatrier.

Combien d'ateliers dans la France même, moins nombreux, mais presque aussi funestes![7]

Diderot saw no alternative to the exploitive wage-relation, but hoped for some regulation of it. And he was a more consistent utilitarian than Bentham was to be, for he held that a smaller net product equally distributed is better than a larger net product so unequally distributed as to divide people into rich and poor classes.[8] Diderot saw no way out of the contradiction between the wage relation and human values, but at least he saw the contradiction.

Burke, who insisted that there was a natural functional order of subordination between labourers and capitalists, and wrote that 'the laws of commerce . . . are the laws of nature, and consequently the laws of God',[9] made capital accumulation the *sine qua non* of civilization. He recognized, in words very like Diderot's, the exploitation inseparable from it, but he would permit no interference with it. Referring to 'the innumerable servile, degrading, unseemly, unmanly, and often most unwholesome and pestiferous occupations, to which by the social economy so many wretches are inevitably doomed', he insisted that it would be 'pernicious to disturb the natural course of things, and to impede, in any

[7] *Réfutation d'Helvétius, Oeuvres complètes de Diderot*, éd. Assezat (Paris, 1875), II. 430-1.

[8] *Encyclopedie*, art. 'Homme (politique)'.

[9] *Thoughts and Details on Scarcity, Works* (Oxford World's Classics, 1907), VI. 22.

degree, the great wheel of circulation which is turned by the strangely-directed labour of these unhappy people.'[10]

Bentham similarly did not mince matters. 'In the highest state of social prosperity,' he wrote, 'the great mass of citizens will have no resource except their daily industry; and consequently will be always near indigence . . .'[11] It was the fate of those without property to be so used. This was the inevitable outcome of the fact that 'human beings are the most powerful instruments of production, and therefore everyone becomes anxious to employ the service of his fellows in multiplying his own comforts. Hence the intense and universal thirst for power; the equally prevalent hatred of subjection.'[12] And Bentham was clear that security of property must have priority over the claims of equality: 'When security and equality are in conflict, it will not do to hesitate a moment. Equality must yield.'[13] This was in spite of the fact that Bentham had shown that, by the principle of diminishing utility, aggregate utilities would be maximized by complete equality of property. But equality was incompatible with capital accumulation and hence with maximization of wealth.

If I might venture a slight digression, I should say that Bentham had done the same thing as the neo-classical economists were to do at the end of the nineteenth century. As Joan Robinson has pointed out about Marshall *et al.*:

The method by which the egalitarian element in the [marginal utility] doctrine was sterilized was mainly by slipping from *utility* to physical output as the object to be maximized. A small total of physical goods, equally distributed, admittedly may yield more *utility* than a much larger total unequally distributed, but if we keep our eye on the total of goods it is easy to forget about utility.[14]

This is just what Bentham had done. Security of property, he argued, must be put ahead of equality because security is necessary to maximize physical output, not utility: he did not notice that he had slipped from one to the other.

With James Mill we touch the high point of recognition of the exploitive nature of market society, though he fetched it from a principle of human nature which he held to be universal 'The desire . . . of that

---

[10] *Reflections on the Revolution in France* (Pelican Classics edn., 1968, p. 271).
[11] *Principles of the Civil Code*, Part I, Ch. 14, § 1.
[12] *Economic Writings*, ed. Stark (1954), III. 430.
[13] *Principles of the Civil Code*, Part I, Ch. 11, para. 3.
[14] *Economic Philosophy* (London, 1962), p. 55.

power which is necessary to render the persons and properties of human beings subservient to our pleasures, is a grand governing law of human nature . . . The grand instrument for attaining what a man likes is the actions of other men.'[15] So everyone seeks exploitive power over others. This view is not carried into his formal economic analysis of wages and profits. But there is in his *Elements of Political Economy* a suggestive passage about slave labour and wage labour.

The only difference [between the manufacturer who operates with slaves and the manufacturer who operates with free labourers] is, in the mode of purchasing. The owner of the slave purchases, at once, the whole of the labour which the man can ever perform: he, who pays wages, purchases only so much of man's labour as he can perform in a day, or any other stipulated time. Being equally, however, the owner of the labour, so purchased, as the owner of the slave is of that of the slave, the produce, which is the result of this labour, combined with his capital, is all equally his own.[16]

Mill's readers would assume that the slave relation was wholly exploitive. For Mill to say, then, that the only difference between it and the wage relation is in the mode of purchasing, is to leave a pretty plain implication that the wage relation is equally exploitive.

It may be noted that, in this catalogue of classical liberal theorists, those who held most strongly that society was necessarily contentious and hence exploitive—namely, Hume, Bentham, and James Mill—asserted this of society as such, not just of capitalist society. But they were able to assert it to be inherent in any society only because they had put into the very nature of man the motivations of bourgeois man. Hume deduced the necessary opposition of passions and consequent opposition of actions from a postulate of insatiable material desire: 'This avidity alone, of acquiring goods and possessions for ourselves and our nearest friends, is insatiable, perpetual, universal . . .'[17] James Mill's 'grand governing law of human nature' takes this a step further, as does Bentham's self-evident proposition, already quoted, that because human beings are the most powerful instruments of production, everyone tries to use everyone else. And Bentham brought this to a finer point by making the pleasure of acquisition stronger than the pleasure of possession. 'It is the pleasure of acquisition, not the satisfaction of possessing, which gives the greatest delights.'[18] Possession is of course

15 *Government*, § IV, ed. Barker (Cambridge, 1937), p. 17.

16 *Elements*, Ch. 1, § 2, in *Selected Economic Writings*, ed. Winch (1966), p. 219.

17 *Treatise*, Bk. III, Part 2, Sect. 2, in *Hume, Theory of Politics*, ed. F. Watkins (1961), p. 41.

18 *Principles of the Civil Code*, Part I, Ch. 6; in *Theory of Legislation*, ed. C. K. Ogden, p. 105.

needed to consolidate acquisition, and is helpful as a means to further acquisition.

Thus all three theorists read back into human nature their observation of bourgeois man—man as infinite appropriator. Having done this, and having made this the reason why government was necessary, they saw no need for further explanation nor any need to make excuses for the social relations it produced.

I find, then, in the classical liberal tradition from Locke to Bentham and James Mill, an increasing recognition of the exploitative nature of a society based on the capital/wage-labour relation, and a corresponding increase in the extent to which the job of the state was thought to be set by economic relations.

With John Stuart Mill and T. H. Green (and their twentieth-century liberal followers) there is a remarkable change. There is in them no recognition, indeed there is a denial, of the exploitative nature of capital; and there is correspondingly a decline in the extent to which the job of the state was thought to be set by economic relations.

It may seem strange to take John Stuart Mill as the watershed, as the beginning of a declining economic penetration of political theory. For in no other theorist is there such a massive relation between political theory and political economy: no one wrote more about both, or linked them so deliberately. But the link is not direct: both are linked to social philosophy. And it was a social philosophy which departed from the utilitarian tradition precisely in its denial that all human values could or should be furthered by or reduced to the market: that was the upshot of Mill's introduction of qualitative differences in pleasures. Mill was concerned to rescue human values from their then subordination to the market. The job of the state was not to facilitate an endless increase in the production of wealth but to fashion a society with higher ends. He was thus, we might say, opposed in principle to the economic penetration of political theory.

At the same time he failed to see that the wage/capital relation was by its nature extractive or exploitive. He saw indeed the exploitation in nineteenth-century society, and denounced it in the strongest terms. Nothing was more unjust than the prevailing relation between work and reward, by which the produce of labour is apportioned

almost in an inverse ratio to the labour—the largest portions to those who have never worked at all, the next largest to those whose work is almost nominal, and so in a decreasing scale, the remuneration dwindling as the work grows harder and more disagreeable, until the most fatiguing and exhausting bodily labour cannot count with certainty on being able to earn the necessaries of life . . .[19]

But he insisted, as did T. H. Green, that this was not inherent in the capital/labour relation, but was due to something else—the original (feudal) forcible seizure of the land, and the failure of subsequent governments to counteract its effects. He even argued that 'industry' has for many centuries been modifying the work of force (ibid.).

Thus, where the earlier liberals had seen that capitalist profit was a deduction from labour's production, but had seen no need to reconcile this with a principle of equity because the system led to increased wealth all around, Mill rejected wealth as the criterion, insisted on a principle of equity, preferred a stationary economy to the rat-race of his contemporary society, but did not see that the prevailing inequity, and the trampling and elbowing, were inherent in the capitalist relation.

It is not just that he did not put exploitation into his economic theory of the determinants of wages and profits. No more, as we have noticed, did Adam Smith or James Mill. But in their cases it was because they made the wealth of the nation the grand criterion, and assumed the inevitability of existing classes, so did not see any need to justify or excuse the prevailing distribution. John Stuart Mill did see that that distribution was not automatically justified. He was the first of the liberals to see this, and to say it. He saw that there was a gap between his idea of maximized utility and the actual utilities that were produced by the class-divided society of his time. He saw that there was something to be explained. But he could not explain it except by denying that the exploitive relation was inherent in the capitalist relation.

Some would argue that Mill's well-known disjunction between the laws of production and the pattern of distribution[20] was his answer to, or his way of avoiding, the difficulty that a competitive market economy in which every bargain was entirely fair would result in a distribution which was utterly inequitable. If this disjunction was intended as such, it was a very poor logical resolution of the difficulty. For the disjunction he made was not between the social relations of production and the social distribution of the product, but merely between the physical laws (e.g. of the fertility of the soil, and hence diminishing returns on increasing applications of labour to the same land) which limit production in any system, whatever are the social relations of production, and

[19] *Principles of Political Economy* (Toronto and London, 1965), Bk. II, Ch. 1, § 3 (*Collected Works*, II. 207).
[20] *Principles*, Bk. II, Ch. 1, § 1 (*Works*, II. 199–200).

any particular system of social distribution. His disjunction was perfectly valid, but it did not meet the difficulty. He simply did not see that capitalist production entailed capitalist distribution, or that the distribution was a co-requisite of the production. Instead, he attributed the inequity of the existing distribution to an historical factor extraneous to the system of production.

Accordingly, he did not see that men's economic relations set the requirements of the political system. In moving away from utility, by redefining it qualitatively, he moved his political theory away from political economy. And T. H. Green, starting from a different base, came full circle back to the Greek ideal of the good life as something apart from and even opposed to material maximization.

This retreat from economic assumptions was not, I think, simply coincidental with the failure to see the necessarily exploitive nature of capitalist productive relations. Both were perhaps due to a third factor: the increasingly evident incompatibility, in the nineteenth century, between the dehumanizing actual economic relations and any morally acceptable vision of a human society. All political theorists, not least those in the liberal tradition, have some vision of human needs and human excellence, and hence a vision of a humanly desirable society. Incompatibility between the exploitive nature of capitalist market relations and a humanistic ethic had not been a serious problem for the seventeenth- and eighteenth-century political theorists. They could, and did, square the massive inequality of the accumulative society based on free contract and wage-labour with a humanistic vision, by pointing out that the market society raised and could continue to raise the general level of material well-being. Since they saw this as a *necessary* condition of moral and cultural improvement, they did not look too closely at the question whether it was also a *sufficient* condition for that improvement.

But by the middle of the nineteenth century this would no longer suffice. The quality of life for the mass of the people in that unequal society had become so blatantly wretched that it could no longer be excused by the ability of the system to go on increasing the national wealth. Sensitive liberals such as Mill found the condition of the working class morally insupportable. Mill's way out, as we have seen, was to attribute the evil to something other than the capitalist relation.

But now we must notice another factor which contributed to the liberal change of position. Not only did sensitive liberals find the conditions of the working class insupportable. So did some emerging working class movements which were making their weight felt politically. There

116 *The Rise and Fall of Economic Justice*

was thus an objective factor, a factor beyond the subjective humanistic perception of sensitive liberals, and it was the objective change that sparked the subjective one. Mill, writing in 1845 of the effects of the Chartist movement, which he described as 'the revolt of nearly all the active talent, and a great part of the physical force, of the working classes, against their whole relation to society' said that 'among the more fortunate classes . . . some by the physical and moral circumstances which they saw around them, were made to feel that the conditions of the labouring classes *ought* to be attended to, others were made to see that it *would* be attended to, whether they wished to be blind to it or not.' He concluded: 'It was no longer disputable that something must be done to render the multitude more content with the existing state of things.'[21]

This suggests that my third hypothesis can be taken one step further. Hypothesis 3 was that the penetration of political theory by economic ideas varies with the theorists' recognition of the necessarily exploitive or extractive nature of market relations in a society divided into owners and non-owners of productive material property. What may be thought a weakness of that hypothesis is that it merely relates one mental operation with another: the theorist's admission of economic assumptions with his *perception* of a certain inherent relation in society.

But now, if my point about Mill is right, we may substitute an external factor for that perception. Instead of a theorist's perception of the inherent exploitiveness of the capitalist relation, we may look to the *exploited class's* perception of its exploitation, and its consequent political action. Thus, for liberal theory, we would have the following proposition: the economic penetration of political theory varies *inversely* with the political strength of an exploited class. And, of course, for socialist theory, which speaks in the name of the exploited class, the economic penetration of the political theory would be expected to vary *directly* with the political strenght of an exploited class.

We may frame this as *Hypothesis 4: That the economic penetration of political theory varies with the political strength of an exploited class; directly in socialist theory, inversely in liberal theory.* This hypothesis is borne out pretty well in both traditions.

In the socialist tradition, Marx may fairly be regarded as the high point of economic penetration of political theory, and his was the period of maximum political strength of class-conscious working-class action in

21 *The Claims of Labour,* in *Dissertations and Discussions,* II. 188–90; and in *Collected Works* (1967), IV. 369–70.

the Western nations. Revisionist and Fabian theory, and subsequent democratic-socialist theory, have corresponded with (and no doubt contributed to) declining class-conscious political action.

In the liberal tradition the inverse correspondence is fairly clear for the seventeenth to nineteenth centuries, in the line I have already sketched: the economic penetration increasing from Locke to Bentham, a period when the threat from below was at least quiescent if not decreasing—(it is true that Burke and Malthus saw a threat in the repercussions of the French Revolution, but Bentham and Ricardo and James Mill did not); then, from John Stuart Mill on through the rest of the nineteenth century, the economic penetration decreasing as the threat from below increased.

What about subsequent liberal tradition? I see, in the twentieth century, a continuation of that line. From Ernest Barker and A. D. Lindsay and John Dewey to, say, Maurice Cranston and John Rawls,[22] the economic penetration of liberal political theory has decreased. And its decrease is correlated with an increase in the apprehended threat to bourgeois liberal societies, not so much a threat by any *indigenous* class-conscious exploited class (for these have not amounted to much in the economically advanced Western nations in this century) but by the global threat of the socialist and Third World societies. It would be astonishing if liberal theorists in countries which, either directly, or indirectly as client states or nostalgic states, rely on global exploitation, did not respond, even if only subconsciously, to the threat. I see them as having done so, and hence as bearing out Hypothesis 4.

It may be objected that I have contradicted myself in referring the twentieth-century change in the Western *socialist* tradition to a *decline* in the political strength of the exploited, and the change in the *liberal* tradition to an *increase* in the threat from those presently or formerly transnationally exploited; it may be thought that the distinction I have made between indigenous and transnational threats is too artificial to hold my case together. But we may see a further unifying factor here, namely, the increasingly uncertain viability of capitalist society. The perception of this by liberal theorists makes them retreat from economic penetration to idealism. The same perception by socialist theorists in the affluent countries easily leads them to think that capitalism cannot keep going without submitting to steadily erosive reforms, and so leads them to press for concessions rather than confrontation, and to bend

[22] Cf. my 'Rawls's Models of Man and Society', *Philosophy of the Social Sciences* (Dec. 1973), pp. 341–7.

their theory towards reformism, with some lack of economic penetration.

I doubt if this explanation can be pressed very far, at least without a good deal of refinement and qualification. And since it concerns only the twentieth century (and only some developments within that time-span) it cannot serve as a general hypothesis. But it does suggest one further general hypothesis which is applicable to the whole rise and fall of the economic penetration of political theory from the seventeenth century on. If we look back over that stretch, which comprises the emergence and maturation and faltering of capitalism, we may entertain the idea, as *Hypothesis 5, That the economic penetration of political theory varies with the theorists' confidence in the ability of an emerging or established economic order to maximize human well-being and to achieve or maintain political dominance.* This may be said to hold both for the rise and decline of the economic penetration of liberal theory from the seventeenth century till now, and for its decline in Western socialist theory from Marx till now. It also appears to hold for the continuance and revival of Marxism in the non-Western world in this century.

The same weakness might be seen in this hypothesis as was seen in Hypothesis 3, namely, that it merely relates one mental operation to another—the theorists' use of economic assumptions with their confidence in some actual or possible economic relations. It would no doubt be tidier if we could reduce the latter to some external factor such as the actual performance of an economic system. We can do so in part, but not entirely.

An improving performance is indeed apt to bring increasing confidence in an existing system. And a faltering performance is apt to bring decreasing confidence in an existing system by its beneficiaries. But the faltering performance of an existing system also brings an *increasing* confidence, by its *non*-beneficiaries, in the possibilities of what they see as an emerging alternative system. This I take to have been as true of Adam Smith as of Marx.

To put the point most generally, confidence in an established or emergent economic system is not reducible to any external factor, because the possibility of an emergent one depends partly on people's perception of such new possibility. I do not see any determinate relation between actual performance and such perception. There are time-lags. There are variations induced by the operation of the system itself. There are different perceptions, by different sections of the community, of the relative value of aggregate affluence and general quality of life. Opinion in one nation may be compelled by changes outside to make a different valuation of the limits of the prevailing system and the possibility of alternatives.

All these things may be seen as happening in our own day. Even some economists have begun to count the cost of economic growth. An optimistic view is that quality of life will get the upper hand, and that we will move away from a society permeated by market behaviour and material maximization. If my first hypothesis still governed then, the economic penetration of political theory would decline. But we should not expect a constant ratio to be maintained during such a move. At the theoretical end-point we might indeed expect it: with zero market there would presumably be zero economic penetration of political theory, if only because there would be zero political economy. Indeed, if, as I suppose, the full transcendence of market behaviour requires an end of scarcity, might there not in that case be zero political theory? That is the logical conclusion that would follow from the postulates of classical liberal theory, which tied political obligation, rights, and justice to scarcity; as Hume put it: 'it is only from the selfishness and confined generosity of men, along with the scanty provision nature has made for his wants, that justice derives its origin . . . it is evident that the . . . extensive generostiy of man, and the perfect abundance of everything, would destroy the very idea of justice . . . because they render it useless.'[23]

However that may be—and it is surely not just one's professional bias as a political theorist that makes one resist the notion of the end of political theory—any move from a market-dominated society to a non-market-dominated society will clearly need the services both of political theory and political economy. And it will need a political theory that recognizes the determining role of necessary and possible relations between people as producers. If need always brought forth what is needed, we would be sure of a continued presence, indeed a revival from the present low point in Western political theory, of economic penetration. But if demand creates supply, we should still have to ask, whose demand? and the answer might not be very encouraging. Or if supply creates demand, we are no better off, for economic thought of the fundamental sort needed by political theory is now in rather short supply. The conclusion which seems inescapable is that we ourselves as political theorists will have to augment the supply, and take the lead in restoring to political theory the economic insight it once enjoyed.

[23] *Treatise of Human Nature*, Bk. III, Part , § 2 (in F. Watkins, ed.), pp. 45-6.

CHAPTER 10

Democracy, Utopian and Scientific[1]

When Engels published his *Socialism, Utopian and Scientific* in 1880, European socialism was in some disarray. He hoped to put it on the right track by making his readers think again about the then competing doctrines of socialism. Now, a century later, European and American democracy is in such disarray that it is tempting to consider whether a parallel analysis of democratic theory could usefully be made.

Engels's division of socialist theory into utopian and scientific had the merit of throwing into bold relief the kind of theory required for moving ahead to a society more humanly acceptable than nineteenth-century capitalism. Can a division of democratic theory into utopian and scientific point us a way ahead now to something more desirable than our present precarious Western democratic systems? It seems a promising starting-point for anyone who is looking for an improved democratic theory as a guide to a better democratic society. If utopian is taken to mean, as Engels used it to mean, nobly intentioned, but unrealistic and therefore ineffective, then clearly those who want a change for the better must avoid the utopian and embrace the scientific.

We should, however, beware of that division into utopian and scientific when we reflect that the twentieth-century liberal-democratic theory which makes most claim to be scientific and most denigrates earlier theory as utopian, concludes that no significant change for the better is possible. Its 'science' tells us to stop dreaming and to be content with the democracy we have. One may suspect that there is something wrong with a distinction between utopian and scientific which makes the two terms mutually exclusive. There is perhaps a simple logical fallacy here: all utopian (i.e. unscientific) thought is visionary, therefore all visionary thought is utopian (i.e. unscientific). The conclusion is surely false, for scientific thought also is visionary.

If we allow that empirical science and scientific vision are not incompatible, we shall have to be wary of Engels's division between utopian

[1] First published in *After Marx*, ed. Terence Ball and J. Farr (Cambridge University Press, 1984).

and scientific theory. For although he, like Marx, did not treat the empirical and the visionary as incompatible, he did lend some support to those who were to take that line later. For he drew the distinction between utopian and scientific theories entirely in economic terms: Marx's theory was scientific in so far as it was based on the advance Marx made in economic science over the classical economists. What Engels forgot, in making his case for Marx's theory at that particular political conjuncture, was that Marx's economic science was pre-eminently a *political* economy.

However, although Engels may be faulted for having reduced Marx's political economy and his political vision to narrowly economic terms, we may still hope to learn something from the contrast he drew between utopian and scientific theory.

Let us explore this by looking first at his criteria for distinguishing them from each other. He reduced the difference between the utopian theories (Fourier, St. Simon, Owen) and the scientific theory (Marx) to two points on which he held that Marx had surpassed all earlier socialist theory. (1) Whereas the utopians had based their theory on abstract ideas of truth, reason and justice 'independent of time, space, and the historical development of man'[2] and had tried to evolve a solution to the social problems 'out of the human brain',[3] Marx had insisted that socialist theory be based on the real, historically changing, power relations of society, which were essentially economic relations. In short, Marx's first surpassing insight was to have seen that the power relations of existing society were transient, that they were a historical stage governed by its own internal laws of motion.

(2) The second and equally important respect in which Marx had surpassed the earlier theory was in discovering the mechanism of exploitation inherent in capitalist society. The utopians had vigorously denounced the exploitive character of the nineteenth-century society, but had been unable to explain it. Marx had discovered the secret of capitalist exploitation, and had formulated it in his law of surplus value.[4]

Thus for Engels the two requirements of a scientific theory of socialism were (1) that it saw existing economic relations to be a transient historical stage, subject to its own internal laws of motion, and (2) that it comprehended and explained the necessarily exploitive nature of those relations.

[2] Engels, *Socialism, Utopian and Scientific*, Chicago, n.d.[1908], p. 74.
[3] Ibid., p. 58.   [4] Ibid., pp. 92-3.

Now if we were to take Engels as our model for assessing the scientific quality of democratic theory we should have to look for *parallel* insights into the *political* relations of existing society. We should have to ask how far, if at all, democratic theory has (1) seen the political relations of existing society as a transient historical stage with its own inherent laws of motion, and (2) understood the necessarily exploitive nature of those political arrangements.

To formulate the question in that way is already to expose its untenable narrowness. For there is no reason to expect that a political system as such, unrelated to the economic system which must serve it and which it must serve, will have its own inherent laws of motion, or its own inherently exploitive character (indeed, to assume that democratic institutions are exploitive in themselves would be to foreclose the question whether liberal democracy can survive exploitive capitalism or even be the mechanism for transcending it).

But if we must abandon a political analogue of Engels's narrow economic criteria, we may still give a central place to laws of motion taken more broadly. We may take as a test of the scientific quality of a democratic theory the extent to which it sees inherently interdependent forces of economic and political change as setting the direction and limits of democracy. After all, neither an economic nor a political system can exist independently of the other. Strains or inadequacies in either will create problems for the other. The worry now in our Western democracies is not about democracy *per se* but about *capitalist* democracy: neo-conservative[5] and neo-Marxist[6] analysts are agreed that there is a crisis of liberal democracy and that the crisis arises from an increasing misfit between demand and supply, that is, between the increasing political demand for the goods of the welfare state and the decreasing ability of the capitalist economy to supply them. No clearer case for presuming the interrelation of political and economic forces need be offered.

So instead of asking how far democratic theory has thought in terms of laws of political motion and political exploitation, we may ask how far it has thought in terms of laws of political-economic motion and political-economic exploitation. We may ask both questions of pre-liberal (seventeenth- and eighteenth-century) as well as liberal (nineteenth- and twentieth-century) democratic theories.[7] I shall first look

[5] e.g. Samuel Huntington, Daniel Bell.

[6] e.g. Jürgen Habermas, Claus Offe, James O'Connor.

[7] On the distinction between pre-liberal-democratic theory (e.g. Rousseau and Jefferson) and liberal-democratic theory (from Bentham and Mill to the present) see my *The Life and Times of Liberal Democracy* (Oxford, 1977), Ch. 1.

very summarily at some highlights of both periods down to the mid-twentieth century, then look more closely at the subsequent and now prevalent theory.

(1) Democratic theorists of both periods have commonly seen the political relations of their own societies as a product of historical change, at least in the obvious sense of seeing that they had emerged from something different, but none saw that change as due to some inherent laws of motion, or thought of such laws as still at work within the existing political system in such a way as to lead to that system being superseded. Pre-liberal democrats, notably Rousseau, confronted with a wholly undemocratic society, did demand that it should be surpassed by something democratic, but had no clear idea *how* it could be surpassed, that is to say, no idea of any inherent laws of motion that might make its supersession possible or probable. Rousseau called for a *deus ex machina*, a charismatic legislator.

In the nineteenth century, liberal democrats, at least those in countries which had already achieved some measure of democratic government, had no interest in enquiring into laws of motion of political society, for they thought the motion had virtually stopped or would stop with the achievement of a substantially representative governmental system, and saw no need to surpass it. John Stuart Mill may be cited as the outstanding liberal democrat in the English tradition. It is true that Mill, following the insight of the classical economists, did see a law of motion of the capitalist economy whereby it would necessarily decline to a stationary condition of no growth, but he did not relate this to a possible decline in the democratic character of the political system: rather, he applauded the prospect of 'the stationary state' as an opening for a more humanistic society. And while he held that there had been some improvement in Western political institutions with the broadening of the franchise, and might be more improvement with some further adjustments of the franchise and other parts of the mechanism, he was content enough with the main lines of existing representative government that he did not think in terms of surpassing it. The existing system, with some adjustments, was about as democratic as could realistically be expected. There was no thought that it ought to be superseded, or that any laws of motion might lead to its supersession. Subsequent liberal-democratic theory has generally followed Mill in that respect.

(2) Our second question is whether any of the democratic theorists have understood the necessarily exploitive nature of the political structure of existing societies. The pre-liberal democratic theorists (Winstanley,

Rousseau) saw clearly that the political institutions of the blatantly class-divided societies in which they lived had as their main function the enforcement of class exploitation. And liberal-democratic theorists who wrote before any measure of democratic institutions had been achieved (e.g. Bentham) were equally clear that the political systems they confronted were essentially exploitive in that they maintained the power of the great proprietors of land and capital to exploit all the rest of the society. But from the time that formal democratic institutions were achieved, liberal-democratic theorists have not generally seen capitalist democratic political institutions as similarly exploitive. Indeed the very idea that they might be so, by virtue of their maintaining and lending legitimacy to an exploitive economic system, is scarcely entertained by liberal-democratic theorists, for they do not generally consider capitalism to be necessarily exploitive.

In this summary account, democratic theory—particularly twentieth-century liberal-democratic theory—comes off badly. It neither thinks in terms of laws of motion nor recognizes exploitation. It fails because it does not give attention to the interrelation between economic and political motion.

But we have still to look at the school of liberal-democratic theory that has become dominant since the mid-twentieth century, which makes some claim to be scientific in that it is based on empirical observation and analysis of the actual functioning of Western democratic systems and does explain how they operate and what forces move them. I refer to the pluralist—élitist—equilibrium theory of Schumpeter, the early Robert Dahl, the voting-studies specialists, and a whole host of followers.

They define democracy narrowly as simply a method of choosing and authorizing governments, and see the democratic political process as a market-like process in which the self-chosen leaders of political parties are the entrepreneurs offering competing parcels of political goods (leaders whose skill lies in estimating the plural demands of the voters), and in which the voters are the consumers whose role is simply to choose which parties' promised parcels they will buy at election time (and in between elections to keep the successful parties up to their promises by acting in plural pressure groups). This is said to produce an equilibrium between political demand and supply, as evidenced by the fact that, at least when all the players stay within the conventional rules of the game, the system does not break down into dictatorship or military rule or chaos. The additional claim made or implied by these theorists, that it provides some measure of consumer sovereignty and is therefore a good thing, is not strictly part of its scientific claim, and is indeed incompatible with it: as I shall suggest in a moment, the justificatory inadequacy of the theory follows logically from the extent of its scientific accuracy.

How strong is the scientific claim of this theory? We may grant that it does describe fairly accurately the way in which the political system in the developed capitalist democracies does operate: the voters do behave as consumers choosing between packages of political goods offered by competing parties, and the party directorates and managers do perform the entrepreneurial functions of judging what goods will be most in demand and then marketing the packages they have put together. And the theory can readily be made to cover some evident political facts which render the system less than ideally democratic. Thus it can recognize that the market in which the parties compete as sellers is oligopolistic, not perfectly competitive: there are only a few sellers, and consequently they need not be fully responsive to buyers' demands, as sellers in a perfectly competitive market must be. The theory can also accommodate the fact that political parties, as oligopolistic suppliers, can to a considerable extent create the demand: as Schumpeter put it, the people 'neither raise nor decide issues but . . . the issues that shape their fate are normally raised and decided for them';[8] the wishes of the electorate 'are not the ultimate data', the electorate's choice 'does not flow from its initiative but is being shaped, and the shaping of it is an essential part of the democratic process.'[9]

The theory's recognition that the party system is structured in such a way that it need not be fully responsive to the votes' demands, and that it can even determine the demand, does severely damage its justificatory claim that the system provides a substantial measure of consumers' sovereignty but does not impugn the theory's descriptive accuracy. It is because and to the extent that the theory recognizes the imperfectly competitive nature of the party system that it can claim some scientific accuracy, but in so far as it does so it must logically give up much of its justificatory claim.[10] A measure of its scientific accuracy is the extent to which it takes as the model of the democratic political system the reality of a mature oligopolistic capitalist economy rather than the simple textbook model of a fully competitive economy.

[8] Joseph Schumpeter, *Capitalism, Socialism, and Democracy* (New York, 1942), p. 264.
[9] Ibid., p. 282.
[10] The equilibrium political theorists differ in the extent to which they recognize the imperfect party competition and to which they claim some measure of consumer sovereignty. On this, see my *The Life and Times of Liberal Democracy*, pp. 81-2.

All that I have said so far about the equilibrium theory gives it some scientific credit, but does not establish it as an adequately scientific general theory of liberal democracy, let alone of democracy as a whole. (I do not here deal with any such broader claim,[11] since the scientific claim of the equilibrium theory is tenable only in respect of existing Western liberal democracies: its narrow definition of democracy as merely a mechanism for choosing and authorizing a government rules out any idea of democracy as a kind of society embodying equality of chances of a fully human life, i.e. rules out something that a scientific general theory of democracy as a whole would have to accommodate. The equilibrium theory praises liberty but forgets equality and fraternity.)

The scientific inadequacy of the equilibrium theory as a general theory of liberal democracy is attributable to its lack of a historical perspective. It situated itself firmly in its own time. Its formative period was the decades following World War II, when Western capitalism appeared to have made a stable recovery, and to be capable, for the foreseeable future, of maintaining a satisfactory rate of economic growth and meeting the expectations of the electorate. Even Schumpeter, who held (though not for the same reasons as Marx) that capitalism had a terminal illness, thought it might have another successful run for a further fifty or a hundred years.[12]

The political scientists who developed the equilibrium theory after Schumpeter had much less doubt about the stability of capitalism and the adequacy of their model of capitalist democracy. They easily assumed that Western liberal democracies would maintain such an equilibrium as not to collapse into dictatorship or chaos. They could overlook the many instances in the mid-twentieth century when some had so collapsed, as in Italian and German fascism and military take-overs in other European and Latin-American countries, which came when their economies could not meet popular expectations. They could overlook or discount those failures because the post-war revival of European capitalisms made any repetition of those failures seem unlikely. And that prognosis appeared to be confirmed by the subsequent restoration of liberal-democratic institutions in Spain, Portugal, and Greece. The future of liberal democracy on the equilibrium theorists' pattern seemed fairly secure. But it depended on the assumption that the rate of economic growth would hold up.

[11] On this, see *Life and Times of Liberal Democracy*, pp. 86–91.
[12] Schumpeter, op. cit, p. 163.

The now endemic slow-down of economic growth in the capitalist world as a whole has put the prospects of liberal-democratic institutions in a different light, and has revealed the shallowness of the equilibrium theory. That theory is static. It takes no thought for the possible outcome of a probably increasing inability of the capitalist economy to satisfy the expectations both of the electorate and of the powerful pressure groups in its midst. A scientific theory of liberal democracy would have to consider at least two possible outcomes: that popular movements intent on transforming or transcending capitalism would demand and get more participatory democratic institutions, or that democracy would be effectively destroyed by some kind of corporatist plebiscitarian state. The equilibrium theory consider neither possibility. Yet either outcome would spell the end of the equilibrium theory's scientific claim.

What the equilibrium theorists forgot was that the democratic franchise was won in the first place in most of the present liberal democracies by the irresistible pressures brought against oligarchic regimes by the new industrial working class and/or the farmers or peasants, who had had no effective political voice. Liberal democracy was founded by class pressure against class oligarchy: the democratic franchise was granted to forestall revolutionary activity by the classes which had been created by competitive capitalism. As long as the capitalist economies went on expanding, the democratic upsurge was tamed, chiefly by the operation of the party system, which was then more fluid than it has become since then.[13]

But now, in the measure that the capitalist economy has matured into oligopoly, *and* has begun to slow down to no-growth, the political and economic oligarchy will have to reckon with a new democratic upsurge, this time by the descendants of those who originally demanded and got a political voice. Such an upsurge is to be expected when those descendants come to recognize that they also are subject to an oligarchic regime. They may not appreciate that the two words 'oligarchy' and 'oligopoly' have the same Greek root, indeed they may never use the words, but they are apt to appreciate the real connection. In the measure that they do so, the present ruling oligarchy will, if it is unable to destroy the liberal democratic state (replacing it with some kind of corporatist state), be compelled to submit to a more genuinely democratic participatory system.

The equilibrium theory takes no thought of such a future. It sees that in affluent Western societies the shop assistant dresses in the same style

[13] Cf. *Life and Times*, pp. 64–9.

as the well-to-do; that the industrial worker has his own car and television set, and is apt to be chiefly interested in his leisure pursuits—his football or pigeon-fanciers club, as long as his income allows him that indulgence; that his concern for his income is usually left to his trade union, which seeks to maintain his slice of the pie but does not question the methods of the bakery; that even if his concern extends to some support for a regional economic pressure group or an ethnic or religious or moral or neighbourhood pressure group, all of those still operate within the limits of the accepted economic and political system. The equilibrium theorist concludes that the class-divided society has been permanently replaced by a relatively complacent pluralist society. That is the limit of his science, and it is an increasingly damaging limit.

It might still be argued, in defence of the equilibrium theorists' position, that capitalism, having emerged successfully from the economic debacle of the great depression of 1929 by adopting Keynesian policies, may overcome its present decline by discovering some comparable new rejuvenating principle. But when one notices that the revival from the 1930s to the 1960s depended not just on Keynesianism but also, as is generally acknowledged, on the boost given the economy by World War II and subsequent lesser wars, and, as is less generally acknowledged, by the massive rearmament required by the continuing cold war, some doubts arise. Actual full-scale war has become too dangerous to be used again. And the rearmament budgets required by cold war are already seen to be, and must increasingly be, at the expense of the Keynesian welfare-state measures which have kept capitalism afloat up till now. A further doubt arises if it is acknowledged that the buoyancy of the Western economies in the Keynesian period has depended on their continued exploitation of the Third World peoples. For it seems likely that that exploitation has nearly reached its limit, that is, a limit which could only be surpassed if the Western powers resorted to outright or concealed dictatorship at home as well as abroad. That also would spell the end of the equilibrium theory. I conclude that the equilibrium theory cannot claim more than a very short-run scientific validity.

We should notice finally what may be described as a conservative revision of the equilibrium theory, as in the work of Samuel Huntington[14] and Daniel Bell[15] It does not seek to replace the descriptive content of

[14] Notably his contribution to *The Crisis of Democracy: Report on the Governability of Democracies to the Trilateral Commission* by Michel Crozier, Samuel P. Huntington, and Joji Watanuki (New York University Press, 1975).
[15] *The Cultural Contradictions of Capitalism* (Basic Books, New York, 1976, 1978).

the equilibrium theory, but, as mentioned earlier, it does find a crisis in current Western democracies and sees the crisis as due to the increasing difficulties of capitalism and the increasing demands of the people. It is not complacent about pluralist society or the viability of liberal democratic institutions. It sees plural demands putting an overload on capitalist democratic institutions, and sees democracies becoming ungovernable.

To the extent that the conservative revisionists recognize an impending crisis in capitalist democracy they may be said to be more scientific than the mainstream equilibrium theorists. They do see some inherent motion in the politics of capitalism: they have got beyond the static limits of the earlier equilibrium theory. But it is doubtful if they can be considered to be approaching a scientific theory of democracy, or indeed if they would make such a claim. They foresee an increasing inadequacy of Western party systems and governmental systems, an inability of the systems to go on providing acceptable government or providing government for an acceptable society, a breakdown of liberal democracy as we have known it. They offer us in effect the euthanasia of liberal democracy and of the equilibrium theory. And on their own implicit premiss of an unchanging human nature their sombre conclusions are realistic enough. But in the end it is the static quality of that premiss that renders their theory unscientific. The theory is inadequate as science because it is not visionary. It sees little or no prospect of Western man moving away from his present behaviour as unlimited material desirer. It does not envisage that the demand for material satisfactions might give way increasingly to demand for a better quality of life and of work. But a theory which, although it sees democracy in motion, rules out such a possible basic change in the forces producing that motion, can not be given much of a scientific rating.

We are left then with the position that neither the pre-liberal democratic theorists (Winstanley, Rousseau, Jefferson), nor the early liberal-democratic theorists (Bentham, Mill), nor the twentieth-century followers of Mill, nor the equilibrium theorists, nor the conservative revisionists, may properly be called scientific. They have all failed, in one degree or another, to take account of the necessary and possible forces of change inherent in capitalist democracy.

To say this is not to condemn them all as valueless. On the contrary, all of them have made a useful contribution to our understanding of democracy, however much the claim of some of them to be scientific has to be discounted and however much the others have been dismissed by the scientific claimants as utopian.

My appreciation of the democratic theories prior to the mid-twentieth century equilibrium theory is rather similar to Engels's appreciation of the utopian socialists. He saw much that was good in their theories. He applauded their humanism, the grandeur of their vision, and their moral rejection of existing exploitive society. Their weakness he attributed to their having written at a time when capitalist relations had not yet fully worked themselves out, so that they were unable to grasp the necessary motion of capitalist society, and hence could not see any way ahead except to draw up blueprints of the good society and hope that the blueprints would be so persuasive, by their beauty and symmetry, that men of good will would adopt them and make them into a reality. We may make the same appreciation and critique of the pre-liberal democratic theory, and the liberal-democratic theory of Mill and his followers: they had the humanism and the vision of a better society, but were writing too early to have understood the dynamics of capitalist society.

When we come to the twentieth-century equilibrium theorists there is not the same parallel. They are not evidently utopian. They have eschewed the humanism and vision of the earlier democrats. Nor are they totally unscientific. They have not altogether failed to recognize the change from early to mature capitalism: as we have seen, the more astute of them have taken account of the change from pure competition to oligopoly. Nevertheless there is some parallel between the weakness I have ascribed to them and the weakness Engels found in the utopians. The curious parallel lies in this: the utopians were writing at a time when capitalist relations had not yet fully worked themselves out; the equilibrium theorists have been writing at a time when the *breakdown* of mature capitalism has not yet fully worked itself out, so that they also see no way ahead, indeed see no need for a way ahead, and so are content with the logical beauty of their analysis and with their truncated democratic ideal. The parallel is in their failure to understand the dynamics of capitalist society.

Let us go back to Engels and consider the opening sentences of his *Socialism, Utopian and Scientific*, 'Modern socialism', he wrote (referring to the whole socialist movement),

is, in its essence, the direct product of the recognition, on the one hand, of the class antagonisms, existing in the society of today, between proprietors and non-proprietors, between capitalists and wage-workers; on the other hand, of the anarchy existing in production. But, in its theoretical form . . . like every new theory, modern socialism had, at first, to connect itself with the intellectual stock-in-trade ready to its hand, however deeply its roots lay in material economic facts.

We may find another parallel here with democratic theory, though again not a complete one. The early democratic movement may also be said to be the product of the recognition of the same class antagonism and the same anarchy of production, and its theory too had to be built from an existing intellectual stock-in-trade. So the early democratic theory was utopian, celebrating liberty, equality, and fraternity and postulating an essentially moral rational man, without fully understanding the nature of the class antagonism or of the anarchy of production which were thwarting man in capitalist society.

But after that, the parallel fails. Nineteenth-century democratic theory still failed to see the source of the class antagonism, and hoped it would be overcome by the plural society. And by the twentieth century, the equilibrium theory assumed that the class antagonism *had* been swallowed up by pluralism. As for recognizing and understanding the anarchy of capitalist production, democratic theory appears to have gone backwards between the nineteenth and twentieth centuries. Yet there is some excuse for the twentieth-century equilibrium theorists, for by their time the anarchy of competitive capitalism to which Engels had referred (where no producers could control the market) was giving way to the increasingly uncompetitive system where collaborating large capitals could control the market and, with some help from the state, could plan and administer it. Capitalist firms, and whole industries, now use the state and at the same time depend on it for favours—subsidies, tax exemptions, contracts, and favourable regulations of many kinds. The capitalist firms and consortiums have in effect become political pressure groups: they compete politically more than economically: and so they can be fitted into the equilibrium theorists' pluralistic political framework. What the theory overlooks is that this is not a very democratic pluralism. To the extent that the equilibrium theory is scientific, it is not democratic. It is neither a utopian nor a scientific theory of democracy. We still have no scientific general democratic theory.

What, then, must we do to move towards one? My analysis here suggests that the most needed step is to work out an adequate theory of the now changing relation between the state and the economy, and project it into the future. We need a new political economy, and we need to develop it without losing sight of the humanistic goals of earlier democratic theory. It was not its humanism that made the earlier democratic theory utopian: it was its faulty political economy. Without a humanistic goal, the scientific enterprise is scarcely worth undertaking; and, if we see beyond the model of market man, nothing but a humanistic vision will make our theory scientific.

CHAPTER 11

Hobbes's Political Economy[1]

I propose here to explore a little farther than I have previously done the way in which Hobbes's economic assumptions entered into, and shaped, his political theory. When I speak of the 'economic assumptions' of Hobbes, or of any other political theorist, I mean his assumptions about the actual and the necessary and the possible relations between people in their capacity as producers and exchangers of the material means of life, and in their capacity as owners or non-owners, and as absolute or conditional owners, of the means of production of the material means of life.

A thinker's conclusions as to what kind of political order is possible will obviously depend on what relations between people he believes are necessary or inevitable. He may base that belief on a metaphysical or theological postulate about the very nature of the universe and hence of man, or he may infer the nature of man from his reading of history and of the relations actually prevailing in the societies he can observe, or on some combination of deduction from metaphysical postulates and induction from observation and history. And I think there is a reasonable presumption that metaphysical postulates themselves are distilled from observed and recorded actual relations between people.

So a theory of what political order is possible, as well as morally desirable, will depend directly or indirectly on the theorist's perception of the actual relations that prevail and have prevailed among men. Among those relations, and not the least important of them, we may expect to find, and we do in fact find even in such Idealist thinkers as Plato and Hegel, the relations I describe as economic relations, that is, the relations between people in their capacity as producers and exchangers of the material means of life.

Needless to say, this approach opens up a field of enquiry far broader than that of twentieth-century economic theory, which generally simply assumes that capitalist market relations are the ideal ones, or are the

[1] First published in *Philosophical Forum*, XIV. 3–4 (Spring-Summer 1983).

necessary ones, or at least are the only ones on which any worthwhile analysis can be based. Modern economists have for the most part forgotten, or believe they have surpassed, the political economy of Adam Smith and the Physiocrats, of Karl Marx and John Stuart Mill. Those 'classical' political economists had seen economic relations as bound up with the political order and political values: they thought of economic analysis as valuable for what it could contribute to the development of social and political principles. Even Mill, whom Marx refused to include among the classical, but designated the first of the 'vulgar' political economists, was still a *political* economist, as witness the subtitle of his *Principles of Political Economy: With some of their Applications to Social Philosophy*.

Some work by historians of economic thought and by unorthodox economists in the last few decades has done something to restore the classical political economists to their rightful place as superior economists, but mainstream twentieth-century economics has been oblivious to such a reassessment.

In parallel with this, twentieth-century analysts and historians of political theory have paid little attention to the economic assumptions of the thinkers they discuss. They have generally taken any such enquiry to be beneath their notice. Yet one need only look at the earliest of the great political theorists, Plato or Aristotle or Aquinas, not to mention such early moderns as Bodin and Grotius, to see that economic assumptions, as I have defined them, entered significantly into political theory long before economics became an independent subject of study. When economics did emerge as a field of enquiry in its own right, it was still closely linked with politics and philosophy. The earliest economists described their subject as political arithmetic or political economy, and the most renowned of them, Adam Smith, a moral philosopher by profession, always regarded economics and politics as branches of moral philosophy. One may notice specific relations between philosophy, politics and economics from that time on[2] though one does not expect to find them discussed much earlier. Where should Hobbes be placed in this respect?

He is generally allowed to be a moral philosopher, and he certainly regarded politics as a branch of philosophy or science. But his political theorizing was completed before any significant work had been published by the early economists, and he did not list economics as another

[2] See my 'The Economic Penetration of Political Theory', above, Ch. 9.

branch of science, so one does not find in his work a discussion of the relation between politics and economics as such.

What one does find, however, is a common source of Hobbes's political concerns and the early economists' economic concerns. The common source was the transformation of English society by the rise of capitalism. Capitalist market relations had already, by mid-seventeeth century, gone far to destroy the traditional society. This required both that some new basis for political obligation be found (which was Hobbes's main concern), and that the traditional role of the state in respect of the economy be reconsidered, to take account of the many new problems that were thrust up by the capitalist takeover (which was the main concern of the early economists, and a secondary concern of Hobbes).

The seventeenth-century economists were for the most part mercantilists, that is to say, were concerned to find what state politics would be most conducive to increasing the productivity and hence the wealth of the nation. They took for granted that state direction and regulation of the economy were required. There was as yet no notion that a self-regulating economy might be feasible: the idea of *laissez-faire* was still a century in the future.

Hobbes too may certainly be counted as a mercantilist: his policy recommendations to the sovereign were all designed to encourage productivity and capital accumulation, and so to increase the wealth of the nation, and of course he insisted that the state should be in charge of all this.

Perhaps it is because Hobbes is so evidently a mercantilist that the essentially capitalist nature of his basic assumptions about the nature of man and society is so generally overlooked. Students of political philosophy nowadays are not usually much acquainted with political economy. They are apt to fall into the common error of identifying capitalism with *laissez-faire*, dating the dominance of capitalism with the Industrial Revolution of the late eighteenth and the nineteenth century, and so treating seventeenth-century mercantilist theory and practice as pre-capitalist. But by any criterion of capitalism used by economic and social historians in both the Marxist and liberal traditions[3] this is a serious error. It leads, naturally, to a failure to consider how far the essentially capitalist assumptions of Hobbes the mercantilist were built into his political theory.

[3] Cf. my *Political Theory of Possessive Individualism*, pp. 48, 58, 62.

I have argued at length elsewhere[4] that Hobbes's assumptions about the actual and the necessary economic relations between his atomized individuals did enter profoundly into his political theory. I believe I have shown that his model of man and his model of society were, though half unconsciously, bourgeois models, and that his use of those models determined his whole argument for the necessity of the Leviathan state. I am not persuaded, by any of the scholarly critiques[5] or less scholarly critiques[6] of that position, that I was wrong.

What I want to do now is simply to refine that interpretation by suggesting that Hobbes's whole argument not only supported the capitalist society whose demands he at least half-understood, but was more specifically (though no more consciously) supportive of that early stage of the capitalist takeover, namely, the period of primary capital accumulation, which had already been in effect long enough for it to have entered his consciousness.

I am not suggesting that Hobbes was consciously writing to support a capitalist take-over: his excoriation of the merchant capitalists, who were then to all appearances the most important ones, and to whose pressures he attributed the civil wars which he deplored,[7] clearly rules out any such intention. And he did not himself distinguish between the requirements of primary capital accumulation and those of capitalist enterprise in general. In any case, the question of conscious intention to support a position, as distinct from what one may, with historical hindsight, see as an objective support of that position, can rarely be conclusively answered.

Nor am I suggesting that it was because Hobbes was a mercantilist, rather than a *laissez-faire* man, that he came out in favour of a Leviathan state. I recognize that seventeenth-century English mercantilism contained significant liberal elements, but then so did Hobbes's doctrine, with its preference for competition as against monopolies, and its assumption that the sovereign would permit market freedoms[8]. And the supreme seventeenth-century liberal, Locke, who was also a

[4] 'Hobbes's Bourgeois Man', in *Democratic Theory: Essays in Retrieval*, Ch. 14; *Political Theory of Possessive Individualism*, Ch. 2: 'Introduction' to Penguin edn. of *Leviathan*, pp. 9–63.
[5] Notably Keith Thomas's in *Hobbes Studies*, ed. Keith C. Brown (1965), pp. 186–236.
[6] William Letwin's, in *Hobbes and Rousseau, A Collection of Critical Essays*, ed. Maurice Cranston and R. S. Peters (1972), pp. 143–64. Cf. my review in the *American Political Science Review*, LXVIII (1974).
[7] As in *Behemoth*, p. 126, as quoted below.
[8] 'the Liberty to buy, and sell, and otherwise contract with one another' etc.; as quoted below (*Leviathan*, Ch. 21, p. 264).

mercantilist, equally recognized the necessity of a sovereign state, objecting only to Hobbes's prescription of a self-perpetuating sovereign.

No line can be drawn between mercantilism and capitalism: mercantilism *was* capitalism, and as such, was nascent liberalism.

With those provisos in mind, we may go on to look a little more closely at Hobbes the political economist. It would be foolish to try to make Hobbes out to be a significant forerunner of the classical political economists, or even of the political arithmeticians of his own century. He did not offer a general theory of exchange value. Nor did he attempt a theory of distribution, i.e., of the determinants of rent, interest, profits, and wages, and the necessary relations between them; nor even a theory of the balance of trade or of foreign exchange.

Nevertheless, his economic assumptions and perceptions are worth more attention than they are usually given. To get at them we should look both at his few explicit statements of a general economic principle and at his many policy recommendations to governments. Both the general propositions and the policy recommendations entail certain assumptions.

(1) The most striking general proposition is the statement (which he took to follow self-evidently from his analysis of the conflictual nature of his model of society):

The *Value*, or WORTH of a man, is as of all other things, his Price; that is to say, so much as would be given for the use of his Power, and therefore is not absolute; but a thing dependant on the need and judgement of another. . . . And as in other things, so in men, not the seller, but the buyer determines the Price. For let a man (as most men do), rate themselves at the highest Value they can; yet their true Value is no more than it is esteemed by others.[9]

We have a threefold proposition:

(a) The value of anything is its market price; there are no non-market determinants or criteria of value.

(b) The value or price of a *man* is what would be given for the use of his power. In a society where wage-labourers were becoming the majority of the labour force (as they were becoming in Hobbes's time[10]), this is to say that the price of labour-power, i.e. the wage, is simply the amount an employer will give for the use of that labour-power.

Marx, in the broadside in which he first drew his famous distinction between labour and labour-power, credited Hobbes, whom he described

[9] *Leviathan*, Ch. 10 (pp. 151-2, Penguin edn.).
[10] See Appendix to *The Political Theory of Possessive Individualism*; and 'Servants and Labourers in 17th Century England', in my *Democratic Theory: Essays in Retrieval*, Ch. 12.

as 'one of the oldest economists and most original philosophers of England', with having already hit on the distinction, which he said, fairly enough, had been overlooked by all subsequent economists until he (Marx) rediscovered and developed it.[11] Marx's tribute was well-deserved. But it perhaps goes a little too far, for there is no evidence that Hobbes thought that what employers would give for the use of labour-power was determined by the cost of maintaining and reproducing the labourer: i.e. that the wage must be enough to do this and could not, in competitive conditions, be more than that. But of course, the whole point of Marx's analysis was that the market value of the labour-power which the capitalist buys is the cost of the labourer's subsistence (and that of his family, to allow for the reproduction of the labour force), whereas his labour-power, when expended, creates more value than that, the surplus value going to the employer as profit and hence as an increase of capital.

(c) The price of a man's power, as of any other commodity, is determined by the buyer, not the seller. The proposition that the prices of *all* commodities are determined by the buyer, not the seller, doesn't make much sense, for Hobbes knew as well as anyone that market prices are jointly determined: 'The value of all things contracted for, is measured by the Appetite of the Contractors . . .'[12] But as a proposition about the price of labour-power in the society Hobbes knew it makes a great deal of sense. Hobbes grew up in Elizabethan and early Stuart England, an England characterized by a large mass of surplus labour, labour made surplus by the sixteenth-century enclosures and the steady erosion of copyhold tenants' customary rights. Hobbes had never known any other society. He could easily assume, therefore, that it was the buyer of labour-power who determined the price.

That he did make that assumption is evident from his caustic remark about merchants and manufacturers

making poor people sell their labour to them at their own prices; so that poor people, for the most part, might get a better living by working in Bridewell, than by spinning, weaving and other such labour as they can do; saving that by working slightly they may help themselves a little, to the disgrace of our manufacture.[13]

The same assumption is implicit in his policy recommendation about

11 *Value, Price and Profit*, § 7.
12 *Leviathan*, Ch. 15, p. 208.
13 *Behemoth*, ed. Tonnies, p. 126.

the able-bodied unemployed:

they are to be forced to work; and to avoyd the excuse of not finding employment, there ought to be such Lawes as may encourage all manner of Arts; as
Navigation, Agriculture, Fishing, and all manner of Manifacture that requires
labour. The multitude of poor, and yet strong people still encreasing, they are to
be transplanted into Countries not sufficiently inhabited . . .[14]

The assumption of an endemic labour surplus is evident.

So we have, in Hobbes's major statement on value, a demand and
supply theory of value in general, and a demand theory of the value of
labour.

(2) A second general proposition may be seen in his assertion that

a mans Labour also, is a commodity exchangeable for benefit, as well as any
other thing.[15]

We should not make too much of this. It is an incidental remark in
a discussion of the uses of foreign trade. Hobbes's point was simply that
a nation which lacked the land and natural resources for primary production could still drive a thriving foreign trade, and increase its power,
by charging for the labour of trading and of working up imported
materials:

And there have been Common-wealths that having no more Territory, than
hath served them for habitation, have neverthelesse, not onely maintained, but
also encreased their Power, partly by the labour of trading from one place to
another, and partly by selling the Manifactures whereof the Materials were
brought in from other places.[16]

The statement, in this context, that labour is a commodity, does not
in itself imply a recognition that the productive labour force was now
mainly wage-labourers, who have to put their labour, rather than its
product, on the market as a commodity. For one part of the labour he
mentions here is the entrepreneurs' labour of trading, and the other part
(the labour of working up imported materials) could be the labour of
independent craftsmen.

We must not assume that Hobbes's concept of a commodity was the
same as Marx's. Hobbes did not define 'commodities' beyond saying
(a) that they are the materials or 'Matter' conducing to life, which men
get from Nature either with or without labour, and (b) that this 'Matter'
includes 'Native' (that which is got within one commonwealth) and

---

[14] *Leviathan*, Ch. 30, p. 387.   [15] *Leviathan*, Ch. 24, p. 295.   [16] Ibid.

'Forraign' (that which is got by importation, in return for exportation of superfluous native matter).[17] So he may here be saying no more than that the labour embodied in the value of exported products has become 'a commodity exchangeable for benefit, as well as any other thing', whether it was the labour of traders or independent craftsmen or wage-labourers.

A commodity, for Hobbes is a material *thing*—any thing which conduces to life or to 'commodious living'.[18] Still, to define a commodity as a material thing, and to see a man's labour as a commodity, is to treat his labour as a material thing, exchangeable in the market, either directly or at one remove.

If we had no other evidence of Hobbes's recognition of the predominant role of wage-labour, his proposition that labour is a commodity would not be conclusive of such recognition. But we have other evidence of his recognition, in the passages quoted above regarding the exploitation of wage-labourers[19] and the recommended treatment of the unemployed.[20] And we may notice that he listed 'taking to hire' as one of the standard contractual relations that needed to be defined by the sovereign.[21] Wage-labour was at least a normal feature of the society Hobbes was prescribing for.

(3) A third general proposition, which is both normative and empirical, embodies a general theory of value:

The value of all things contracted for, is measured by the Appetite of the Contractors: and therefore the just value, is that which they be contented to give.[22]

This abrupt dismissal of the medieval concepts of commutative justice and the just price (which required that only *equal* values could legitimately be exchanged), again reveals Hobbes's recognition that the impersonal market had already taken over from the traditional society which had imposed (or had tried to impose) non-market ethical standards on market transactions. And the premise from which he deduces his doctrine of the just value is set down as a generalization of fact: exchange value *is* measured by the appetites of the exchangers. We have here again a demand and supply theory of value.

[17] *Leviathan*, Ch. 24, first four paragraphs (pp. 294–5).
[18] Ibid., Ch. 13, last paragraph (p. 188).
[19] *Behemoth*, p. 126.
[20] *Leviathan*, Ch. 30, p. 387.
[21] *Leviathan*, Ch. 24, p. 299, as quoted below, p. 143, at n. 37.
[22] *Leviathan*, Ch. 15, p. 208. Cf. *De Cive*, Lamprecht edn., p. 46.

(4) One further general proposition should be noted: one which has suggested to some, I think mistakenly, that Hobbes had a labour theory of value.

As for the Plenty of Matter, it is a thing limited by Nature, to those commodities, which from (the two breasts of our common Mother) Land, and Sea, God usually either freely giveth, or for labour selleth to man-kind.
. . . Plenty dependeth (next to God's favour) meerly on the labour and industry of men.[23]

Similar statements are made in *De Cive*, e.g. 'There be no man but knows, that riches are gotten with industry, and kept by frugality. . . .';[24] and more precisely, prefacing some economic-policy recommendations;

There are two things necessary to the enriching of subjects, labour and thrift; there is also a third which helps, to wit, the natural increase of the earth and water . . . Since therefore, there are three things only, the fruits of the earth and water, labour, and thrift, which are expedient for the enriching of subjects, the duty of commanders in chief shall be conversant only about those three.[25]

Hobbes accordingly recommends policies to promote the increase of the earth and water 'such as husbandry and fishing', laws 'against idleness, and such as quicken industry', and laws against inordinate expenditure on consumables.

All this is consonant with a labour theory of value but it is far from being one. There is no suggestion here that things exchange in proportion to the amounts of labour required to produce them. Indeed in these passages Hobbes is not thinking at all of the determinants of exchange value (as he was in the propositions examined earlier), but only of the means to the enrichment of the citizens and the wealth of the nation. Like other mercantilists, Hobbes was more interested in the wealth of the nation than in the determinants of exchange value. All his policy recommendations are designed to increase the wealth of the nation by promoting the accumulation of capital, as in the recommendations already noticed, and in his taxation policy.[26]

The nation's wealth was to be increased by private enterprisers seeking their own enrichment, which the state should encourage. The benefits which the subjects expected of the sovereign, when they entered the contract which created the sovereign, were precisely described:

The benefits of subjects respecting this life only, may be distributed into four

[23] *Leviathan*, Ch. 24, p. 295.
[24] *De Cive*, Ch. 12, § 9; Lamprecht edn., p. 135.
[25] *De Cive*, Ch. 13, § 14, pp. 150-1.
[26] *Leviathan*, Ch. 30, pp. 386-7; *De Cive*, Ch. 13, §§ 10-11, pp. 147-8.

kinds. 1. That they be defended against foreign enemies. 2. That peace be preserved at home. 3. *That they be enriched as much as may consist with public security.* 4. That they enjoy a harmless liberty.[27]

And in stipulating 'the duties of rulers' and 'the office of the sovereign', Hobbes emphasized that those duties and that office amounted to much more than procuring the physical safety of the subjects.

Now all the duties of rulers are contained in this one sentence, the safety of the people is the supreme law. . . . But by safety must be understood, not the sole preservation of life in what condition soever, but in order to its happiness . . . to furnish their subjects abundantly, not only with the good things belonging to life, but also with those which advance to delectation.[28]

The duty of rulers was to enable the subjects to provide for themselves not merely abundance, but delectation beyond abundance. Similarly in *Leviathan*:

The office of the Soveraign . . . consisteth in the end, for which he was trusted with the Soveraign Power, namely the procuration of the *safety of the people* . . . But by Safety here, is not meant a bare Preservation, but also all other Contentments of life, which every man by lawfull Industry, without danger, or hurt to the Common-wealth, shall acquire to himselfe.[29]

Hobbes grounded the sovereign's right to levy taxes simply on the sovereign's obvious need to raise by taxes a revenue sufficient to protect the individual right to private benefit from each individual's own efforts: 'For the Impositions that are layd on the People by the Sovereign Power, are nothing else but the Wages, due to them that hold the publique Sword, to defend private men in the exercise of severall Trades, and Callings.'[30] Only where the activity of individual enterprisers might have harmful effects on the wealth and strength of the nation was the state to intervene, as in regulation of monopolies,[31] of corporations,[32] and of foreign trade.[33] Other than that, the job of the state was simply to establish the laws of property and of contract. The policy recommendations required of course that the state should have those functions.

Only the sovereign, i.e. the state, could establish the laws of property, for only it could establish the institution of individual property: without

---

[27] *De Cive*, Ch. 13, § 6, p. 144 (emphasis added); cf. *Elements of Law* ed. Tonnies, Part II, Ch. 9, §§ 3–4, p. 143.
[28] *De Cive*, Ch. 13, §§ 2, 4, pp. 142–3; cf. *Elements of Law*, Part II, Ch. 9, § 1, p. 142.
[29] *Leviathan*, Ch. 30, p. 376.
[30] *Leviathan*, Ch. 30, p. 386; cf. *De Cive*, Ch. 12, § 9, p. 136; Ch. 13, § 10, p. 147.
[31] *Leviathan*, Ch. 22, pp. 281–3, and Ch. 29, p. 374.
[32] *Leviathan*, Ch. 29, p. 375.   [33] *Leviathan*, Ch. 24, p. 299.

a sovereign state (i.e. in a state of nature) there could be no *meum* and *tuum*.[34] The laws of property are 'the Rules, whereby every man may know, what Goods he may enjoy and what Actions he may doe, without being molested by any of his fellow Subjects: And this is it men call *Propriety*.'[35] Property, Hobbes saw, was a legal relation between men, not merely a relation between men and things.

Moreover, property, for Hobbes, was the right to exclude others from the 'free use and secure enjoyment [of any thing] at all times, according to your own will and pleasure': 'that which is required to a propriety of goods is not that a man be able to use them, but to use them alone, which is done by prohibiting others to be an hindrance to him.'[36] There was of course nothing novel in Hobbes's defining property as a person's right not only to use, but to exclude others from the use of, some thing. It is true that theorists from the classical Greeks down to as late as Bodin had recognized common property as well as private, but their private property, even though it might be a right only to a limited use of say a parcel of land, was a right to exclude others from that use. So Hobbes's concept of property as an exclusive right was not at all original. It is mentioned here only to draw attention to the striking exception on which he was insistent: individual property is the right to exclude all others *except the sovereign*. This proviso I shall suggest was peculiarly appropriate to the era of primary capital accumulation.

Equally important as the sovereign's function of establishing the laws of property was his function 'to appoint in what manner, all kinds of contract between Subjects, (as buying, selling, exchanging, borrowing, lending, letting, and taking to hire,) are to bee made: and by what words, and signes they shall be understood for valid.'[37] Three things about this deserve emphasis. First, the sovereign, whether king or parliament, is given full power to prescribe the validity or invalidity of every kind of contract, including leases: there is no room left for any of the traditional rights of tenants or any traditional limits on market transactions which the sovereign may wish to override. Secondly it is clear that Hobbes understood the right of individual property to include the right to alienate one's property by selling or exchanging. Thirdly, by his inclusion of 'taking to hire' among the ordinary kinds of contract, he was taking for granted the right to alienate one's labour in a wage

[34] *Leviathan*, Ch. 18, p, 234; Ch. 24, p. 296.
[35] *Leviathan*, Ch. 18, p. 234.
[36] *De Cive*, Ch. 14, § 7, p. 160; cf. *Leviathan*, Ch. 24, p. 296.
[37] *Leviathan*, Ch. 24, p. 299.

contract. And we should notice that Hobbes expected that the sovereign would provide a large measure of individual freedom for all such alienations:

> . . . seeing there is no Common-wealth in the world, wherein there be Rules enough set down for the regulating of all the actions, and words of men, (as being a thing impossible:) it followeth necessarily, that in all kinds of actions, by the laws praetermitted, men have the Liberty, of doing what their own reasons shall suggest, for the most profitable to themselves.

> . . . The Liberty of a Subject, lyeth therefore only in those things, which in regulating their actions, the Sovereign hath praetermitted: such as is the Liberty to buy, and sell, and otherwise contract with one another; to choose their own aboad, their own diet, their own trade of life, and institute their children as they themselves think fit; & the like.[38]

By giving the sovereign the basic functions of establishing the laws of property (which were thus removed from any requirement of conformity to natural law), and the laws of contract and exchange (which assumed that property was alienable), and by making it the duty of the sovereign to promote private enterprise and accumulation, Hobbes was endorsing the death warrant of the limited and conditional property rights that had prevailed previously. His doctrine justified the erosion of the rights of copyhold tenants, which had been upheld until recently by manorial courts, and the enclosure legislation which deprived tenants and cottagers of their rights in the common. The actual revocation of those rights brought much land onto the capitalist market. In justifying this, Hobbes was clearing the way for the triumph of the capitalist economy.

It is sometimes thought that Hobbes's theory of private property rights was defective in that it gave the proprietor no right as against the sovereign. Hobbes was quite clear that there was no such right. Property rights were entirely within the power of the sovereign, since, as we have already noticed, Hobbes held that until the establishment of sovereign power all men had a right to all things. Consequently, 'the Propriety which a subject hath in his lands, consisteth in a right to exclude all other subjects from the use of them; and not to exclude their Soveraign . . .'[39] This seems a weaker claim than the one that was made by Locke some forty years later and which soon became the bourgeois credo. Locke asserted a *natural right* to individual property, a right prior to civil society and government, a right which excluded the exactions of

---

[38] *Leviathan*, Ch. 21, p. 264.
[39] *Leviathan*, Ch. 24, p. 297; *Elements of Law,* Part II, Ch. 8, § 8, p. 138.

any sovereign other than the people themselves or their representatives in Parliament, who could legitimately authorize taxation.

But that forty years made a lot of difference. Hobbes was writing in an economy in which the process of primary accumulation of capital was still of first importance. And he saw that, to facilitate that accumulation, a sovereign power which could cut through all the traditional restraints was needed. If his doctrine seems inadequately protective of private property, it was nevertheless just the doctrine needed in the 1640s and 1650s to clear the way for unlimited capital accumulation. Without acting on such a doctrine the state could not have paved the way for the private property right which a later generation would seek to protect even against the state.

I conclude that Hobbes's doctrine was admirably suited to the period of primary accumulation of capital, and that his perception of the needs of the time not only determined his policy recommendations but also to a considerable extent determined his political theory.

His perception of the new role required of the state in order to promote the enrichment of the citizens and hence the wealth of the nation clearly determined his policy recommendations. The same perception, I suggest, determined his grant to the sovereign of full power to prescribe the laws of property and contract, a power overriding the traditional protections afforded by the common law. And, beyond that, his perception of the state's new role required him to find a new, untraditional, basis for political obligation: none of the old bases were adequate to support the new required role. Thus we may say that Hobbes's economic perceptions set the problem which his political theory was designed to solve.

It was a problem of legitimation. Whereas the central problem of a twentieth-century theory of the state is the legitimation of the 'late' capitalist state, Hobbes's problem was the legitimation of the early capitalist state. He attacked that problem ruthlessly, and his solution was in all but one respect the only logical one. The one feature of his solution which was not logically required was his insistence on a self-perpetuating sovereign body, an insistence which was perhaps already otiose in 1651 and certainly became so by 1689 when the bourgeoisie had shown that it was capable of effective class coherence, albeit in a marriage of convenience with the already considerably bourgeoisified landed gentry and aristocracy. The rest of his solution was logically required by his assumption that the needs of the ascendant bourgeois order could not be denied.

I might add, though it is not essential to the case I am making here, that it was fundamentally only Hobbes's stipulation that the sovereign be self-perpetuating that made his doctrine unacceptable to the bourgeoisie. Everything else which was unacceptable in his doctrine, most notably his insistence on the sovereign's right over individual property, stemmed from that. Liberal theorists, from Locke on, had no objection to the sovereign's right to encroach on individual property *provided that* the sovereign power was exercised by a non-self-perpetuating body of representatives of the property-owning class. Apart from the self-perpetuating stipulation, Hobbes's legitimation theory was largely acceptable in his own time, and it may be said to have remained the mainstay of the capitalist state until our own time. I do not press this view of Hobbes's acceptability. My concern here is with the different question of the extent to which his economic assumptions affected his political theory.

On that question I think it is not too much to say that Hobbes's economic perceptions determined not only his problem but also the central point of the solution he proposed: the need for all citizens to acknowledge obligation to a sovereign untrammelled by traditional restraints.

CHAPTER 12

Hampsher-Monk's Levellers[1]

I welcome the new attention to the political theory of the Levellers in Iain Hampsher-Monk's substantial and closely argued paper.[2] He proposes an alternative interpretation to the one I offered fifteen years ago,[3] which as he says has won a grudging acceptance. An interpretation which has become near-orthodox in fifteen years is certainly due for a fresh look, and he has set about this with great care and attention to detail. I am not persuaded that his reading of the documents should replace mine, but I do think that the issue is important enough to deserve a statement of my reasons for rejecting his view (if only to save him from the fate of becoming the new orthodoxy fifteen years hence), even though this requires something of the same attention to detail that he has given.

His case is in three parts: the first and longest disputing my view that the Levellers were never advocates of manhood suffrage; the second rejecting my reading of the Levellers' concept of property as a reading back into the seventeenth century of a twentieth century concept; and the third offering a reconstruction of the earlier traditional view of the Levellers' political theory as preferable to mine. Let me comment on these in turn.

I

Hampsher-Monk's challenge to my reading of the Levellers' position on the franchise rests on eight grounds.

(a) That Ireton, in opening the debate at Putney on the franchise clause of the First *Agreement* (which called for a distribution of electors between counties, cities and boroughs, more proportional to the number of the inhabitants) said that its wording made him think that it

---

[1] First published in *Political Studies*, 25.4 (1977).

[2] 'The Political Theory of the Levellers: Putney, Property and Professor Macpherson', *Political Studies*, XXIV (1976), 397–422.

[3] C. B. Macpherson, *The Political Theory of Possessive Individualism* (Clarendon Press, Oxford, 1962).

intended a vote for every inhabitant: this, Hampsher-Monk takes (p. 398) to be 'a strong indication' that that was the meaning commonly given up till then to the Levellers' references to the franchise. But it is no such indication, for Ireton gives that as only one of two possible meanings, saying in the same sentence 'if that be the meaning, then I have something to say against it' and in the next sentence 'But if it be only . . . those people [who have it now by the civil constitution] . . . I have no more to say against it' (Woodhouse, *Puritanism and Liberty* (hereafter abbreviated as *W*), p. 52). Thus Ireton is asking, which does the clause mean? The answer, which he gets a moment later from Petty, is, neither: the answer is 'We judge that all inhabitants that have not lost their birthright should have an equal voice in the elections' (*W*, p. 53). This answer of course leaves open the question, who did the Levellers think had lost their birthright? I have argued (*Political Theory of Possessive Individualism* (hereafter *PI*), pp. 124–5), with evidence, that it included servants. Hampsher-Monk simply asserts (p. 399, n. 1), that it refers only to delinquents.

(b) That the Levellers never repudiated imputations by other writers that they stood for manhood or universal suffrage. Four such imputations are cited (p. 398, n. 6). Of these, only the first (Edwards's *Gangraena*, 1646) is relevant, and I think it doubtful that much weight should be given to it, partly for the reason I gave (*PI*, p. 119); the second (*A Declaration* . . .) imputes only a demand for franchise for all 'the free-born people', which as I have argued did not include 'servants while servants'; the third (Walker) dates from 1660, years after the Leveller movement had died; the fourth (Parker) dates from 1650, i.e. after the Third *Agreement* in which the Levellers had explicitly excluded servants and almstakers and had thus already falsified the imputation.

(c) That on more than six occasions in the Putney debate after Rainborough's famous claims for 'the poorest he' and 'any man that is born in England', one or more of the debaters 're-iterates the basis of the issue that divides them' (p. 399 at n. 4). Most of the passages he quotes (n. 4) are by Cromwell or Ireton, who did indeed, as I had pointed out (*PI*, pp. 126–7), repeatedly pose the issue as one between a property and a manhood franchise, and did impute the manhood demand to the Levellers, but this does not mean that the Leveller spokesmen accepted that as the issue. The Leveller statements he quotes, by Rainborough and Clarke, are I think still open to my interpretation (as meaning freeborn men who have not entered voluntary servitude, *PI*, p. 126), and do not imply that they accepted property vs. manhood franchise as the issue. Hampsher-Monk does not controvert the explanation I offered (*PI*, pp. 126–8) of their neglecting to repudiate the imputation at that stage of the debate.

(d) That (pp. 400–1) Ireton must have been taking the Leveller demand to be manhood rather than non-servant franchise for he said that it might destroy property, which a manhood franchise might do but a non-servant franchise could not do because even on my estimates the latter would add only about 205,000 voters (ratepayers etc.) to the 212,000 (freeholders) who had the vote already. The arithmetic is correct, but it would be quite possible (and Ireton would presumably realize this) that the 205,000 non-freeholders could win more than half the seats in Parliament against the 212,000 freeholders. Psephology aside, a near-doubling of the franchise must have seemed menacing to any Grandee.

(e) That (p. 401) the number of voters that would be added by the non-servant franchise over and above what Cromwell and Ireton were prepared to include in the franchise is far less than, indeed only about one-tenth of, the 205,000 difference I found. Hampsher-Monk gets this figure (21,000: it would actually be 42,000, but his point would still stand) by treating Ireton as willing to extend the franchise to all rate-payers: he speaks of 'Ireton's ratepayer franchise' (p. 401). I find no evidence at all for this. The farthest Cromwell was willing to go was to include some 'copyholders by inheritance' (*W*, p. 73), and Ireton, in allowing some enlargement of the franchise as long as it was still confined to those who have a local permanent interest, explicitly excluded all the leaseholders 'upon a rack rent for a year, for two years, for twenty years' (*W*, p. 62), and implicitly (*W*, p. 67) those who had money but no fixed property, i.e. between them, presumably the bulk of the non-freehold ratepayers.

Hampsher-Monk's remark (p. 401, n. 2) that the Heads of *Proposals* and the *Second Agreement* 'suggest ratepayer franchises' does not help his case. The *Heads*, which Ireton was at that point offering as a basis for a settlement, called simply for a redistribution of seats between counties proportional to the rates they bore: this is consistent with any franchise (*PI*, n. J, pp. 296–7). The Second *Agreement*, a year after Putney, did call for a ratepayer franchise, but it was as Hampsher-Monk recognizes (p. 401, n. 2) a compromise document, and as I have argued (*PI*, p. 117) one which the Army leadership probably never intended to adhere to. Hampsher-Monk's assumption (p. 404 at n. 2) that Ireton, in reverting to the *Heads*, was proposing a ratepayer franchise is thus without foundation. And in view of Ireton's explicit exclusion of rack-rent leaseholders, and of Cromwell's admission only of some copyholders by inheritance, it is surely a mistake to treat the franchise they were prepared to admit as anything like a ratepayer franchise.

(f) That (p. 402) Rainborough, in rejecting Rich's argument as 'a fine gilded pill' (*W*, p. 64), was rejecting a suggestion that he should relinquish, not that he should adopt, a stand for manhood suffrage. Rich is indeed pretty clearly imputing a manhood suffrage position to Rainborough, and bringing a new argument against it. But what Rainborough replies to is the argument, not the imputation. His reply, so far as it can be made out from the text (which is unusually defective here) is that if the argument is valid (i.e. if extending the vote to the poor would result in their selling their votes to the rich), then he would rather leave things as they are. Hampsher-Monk's reading of this as an acceptance of the imputation is certainly tenable, and I think now that my reading of Rainborough's apparent preference for 'the people' as against 'the poor' as a 'fairly clear rejection' of the imputation (*PI*, p. 128) was too strong, but the text is too defective at this point to establish a perfectly clear inference.

(g) That the Leveller description (in the *Letter from Several Agitators*) of the committee's recommendation of votes for 'all soldiers and others, if they be not servants or beggars' as a victory for 'this your native freedom' cannot be read as an equation of a franchise excluding servants and beggars with a victory for native freedom generally, since the *Letter* was addressed only to the soldiers, all of whom would be enfranchised (pp. 404–5). Hampsher-Monk is quite correct. I should not have listed this along with the explicit broad equation in *The Grand Designe* and the *Petition* of January 1648 (*PI*, pp. 108–9); though in view of the latter statements it seems likely that the question in the *Letter* was implicitly as broad.

(h) That there were 'three specific assertions of universal right made on the eve of Putney' by the Levellers, viz. the first *Agreement, The Case of the Armie*, and *The Copy of a Letter* (p. 405, n. 5). But none of these is a specific demand for manhood franchise. (i) The *Agreement* called only for redistribution of seats 'according to the number of the inhabitants': this could mean *either* all inhabitants *or* all presently qualified inhabitants (as Ireton saw, *W*, p. 52) *or* something in between; the clearest Leveller statements are that it meant something in between, i.e. a nonservant franchise (*Grand Designe*, and *Petition* of January 1648). (ii) *The Case of the Armie* can only be made to appear to demand manhood suffrage if one uses the Woodhouse printing (*W*, p. 433), but as I pointed out (*PI*, p. 130, n. 2) Woodhouse moved a comma and so altered the sense. The original manuscript reads 'all the free-borne . . . excepting those that have or shall deprive themselves of that their freedome, either for some yeares, or wholly by delinquency'; and as I argued (*PI*, p. 130) the 'for some years' exclusion is likely to have been intended for 'servants while servants'. Hampsher-Monk goes Woodhouse one better by giving us the comma in both places. (The moving comma appears in a still different place in his quotation of the same passage at p. 419.) (iii) *The Copy of a Letter* (11 Sept. 1647) calls for the vote for 'every free man of age'; this leaves open the question whether, as I have argued, the Levellers always assumed, as they did at Putney and later, that servants had forfeited their status as free men.

To conclude this review of the evidence on the Leveller position on the franchise, I do not find that Hampsher-Monk's readings set up a presumption that they were ever advocates of manhood suffrage. The only presumptive evidence of any account is the few apparently unqualified statements by Leveller spokesmen at Putney. These I noticed (*PI*, p. 126 at n. 3), and argued could well be understood to refer only to those who had not lost their freeborn right. I should perhaps have made that argument more forcefully, but I thought and still do think that the evidence for it is strong: quite apart from Petty's statement (at *W*, p. 83), the Leveller *Petition* of January 1648 and Harris's *Grand Designe* (December 1647), both of which I quoted (*PI*, pp. 124, 125) seem to me decisive, and Hampsher-Monk does not seek to controvert their clear equation of 'all the Free-born people' (*Petition*) and 'all persons' (*Grand Designe*) with all except servants and beggars. Nor does he deal with the Third *Agreement's* exclusion of servants and beggars as in accordance with 'naturall right'. So, intelligent and sensitive as is Hampsher-Monk's reading of the nuances of the debate at Putney, I do not think he has made his case or seriously impugned mine. On the evidence, the balance seems to me to remain in favour of my reading of the Levellers' position as a demand for a non-servant franchise rather than a manhood franchise.

II

I can comment much more briefly on Hampsher-Monk's discussion of the use I made of the Levellers' concept of property. Much of what he says about the changing concept of property down to the seventeenth century is not in dispute between us: I had already drawn attention to

152   *The Rise and Fall of Economic Justice*

one central difference between seventeenth- and twentieth-century usage (*PI*, p. 143, n. 3) and had elaborated the differences between pre-seventeenth-century and later usages (*Democratic Theory*, hereafter *DT*, Ch. VI)[4] in terms quite similar to those he now uses (pp. 406–9). I do not think that I can be accused of reading back a twentieth-century concept into the seventeenth century. The difference between us is about the extent to which the modern concept had made its way by the mid-seventeenth century. There is indeed room for further debate about this, but I am content to rest my case for the present on the analysis made in the *Democratic Theory* essay.[5]

At the end of his discussion of the meaning of property Hampsher-Monk refers briefly (p. 412) to the question of the meaning of 'freemen' and 'freeborn'. He quotes Overton's championship of 'old bellows menders, cobblers, tinkers or chimney-sweeps' as 'equally free-borne with the highest and loftiest'. Indeed the Levellers did so regard them. But these were not servants: they were, although at the lowliest level, independent tradesmen (see *PI*, p. 149), and as such had not forfeited their freeborn status.

In a final cast in this section of his article Hampsher-Monk notices two related questions: whether one's free status could be lost by entering into a wage relation, and whether all wage-earners could be described as 'servants'. He does not deal with the first question except to refer the reader to Laslett and other critics of my position, who have not I think doubted that being a servant was a perfect badge of that dependence on the will of others which the Levellers held to disqualify a man for the franchise. On the second question he offers the proposition that the day labourer, as distinct from the contracted or customary servant, was clearly not so dependent, since in a true market society the former 'would have an infinite number of employers to go to'. But as I have pointed out (*DT*, pp. 214–15), in those years of unemployment the day labourer was if anything even more dependent than the wage-earner on annual contract. And I have I think sufficiently shown (*DT*, Ch. XII) that 'servants' generally meant all wage-earners.

III

Hampsher-Monk's concluding section (p. 412–22) is designed (p. 398) as 'a fuller alternative reconstruction of the Levellers' political ideas'.

[4] C. B. Macpherson, *Democratic Theory* (Clarendon Press, Oxford, 1973).
[5] For a more succinct statement of the difference, see my 'Human Rights as Property Rights', above, Ch. 6.

Had he demonstrated a need for an alternative reconstruction, his would be an attractive one. Rejecting what he regards as my reduction of the Levellers' ideas to their concept of self-propriety (a reduction to which I do not plead guilty) he emphasizes their reliance on a law of nature which is a law of reason. I do not question that reliance: it is evident in many passages which he and I quote. They used it, as he points out, to deny the right of King or Parliament to infringe certain natural rights of the individual, and to deduce limits to the rightful power of any constituted authority on the ground that all such power rests on a social contract and that no contract which contravenes the law of nature can be valid. All this is clear. I do not at all dissent from it. But I do not find it in any way inconsistent with, or an alternative to, my reading of the Levellers as prototypes (though with the qualifications which I pointed out, *PI*, pp. 154-8) of the liberal possessive individualism which came to full fruition with Locke. Locke made precisely the same arguments as those of the Levellers' noted by Hampsher-Monk (p. 414 at n. 10, and pp. 415-6), and I do not find it disputed that Locke was a possessive individualist.

Finally it should be noticed that Hampsher-Monk, in making his alternative reconstruction of the Levellers' ideas, admits (pp. 419-20) that they did exclude beggars and servants. This seems to me to give away the whole of the position he took in the first part of his article. The position is not saved by his referring to the exclusion as 'something that may have been conceded on other grounds' (p. 419-20), or as 'a tactical concession' (p. 420), involving only the small groups of itinerant beggars (the almspeople were surely just as, if not more, dependent) and 'domestic servants on long contracts to masters' (there weren't any: they all moved within a year or two; see *DT*, pp. 216 ff.). Apart from that, his initial position is decisively lost by his recognition of the very reasonable reasons why the Levellers should have excluded all beggars and servants, i.e. that both were so dependent on others as to be 'not free to use their reason and follow their conscience' (p. 420). I agree that that was the Levellers' reason for excluding them. But they did exclude them. And I do not see that that ground is greatly different from the ground I offered. Servants were dependent because they had given up, while servants, their birthright freedom; almspeople had been reduced to obvious dependence; itinerant beggars had put themselves outside civil society (*PI*, p. 147). There was thus every reason for the Levellers to exclude them from the franchise, which as I have said and as Hampsher-Monk now apparently agrees, they did.

In view of all this, I am not inclined to accept the charge of historicism which Hampsher-Monk levels at me. I do not think that I have 'impoverished history itself' by reading into the Levellers 'the assumptions of our own society' (p. 421): I have rather tried to show that the received view of the Levellers, which he wishes to reinstate, is itself a product of failing to consider how far market assumptions had penetrated English political thinking by the mid-seventeenth century. On the extent of that penetration there may well be continuing debate, which I shall welcome: until then, charges of historicism seem premature.